# BRITISH HORSE SOCIETY
# EQUITATION

# BRITISH HORSE SOCIETY

# EQUITATION

## Training of
## Rider and Horse
## to Advanced Levels

Country Life
in association with the
British Horse Society

Published by Country Life Books
in association with the
British Horse Society
and distributed for them by
The Hamlyn Publishing Group Limited
London · New York · Sydney · Toronto
Astronaut House, Feltham, Middlesex, England

First published 1982

ISBN 0 600 36827 0

Printed in England by
Fakenham Press Limited, Fakenham, Norfolk

# Contents

# Preface

The British Horse Society's *Equitation* is based on the classical lines first written about by Xenophon (430–354 BC), maintained by the Spanish Riding School in Vienna and now amended for competitions by the Fédération Equestre Internationale.

Whilst it is difficult, if not impossible, to lay down hard and fast rules on the training of the horse and rider, and horsemastership in general, *Equitation* is a concensus of opinion of the national authorities and represents the general view in Britain of equitation and horsemastership.

*Equitation* has been compiled by Jane Kidd and illustrated by Eve Littleton. This book is the result of many eminent members of the British Horse Society devoting a good deal of time voluntarily to discussing and writing about the subject. It is impossible to mention all who have assisted, but the following have made major contributions: Lt-Col J. D. Crawford, F.B.H.S.; Mrs B. Slane Fleming, F.B.H.S.; Geoffrey Hattan, F.B.H.S.; Mrs J. Holderness-Roddam; Mrs H. W. Inderwick; J. Leacock, F.R.C.S.; Mrs A. G. Loriston-Clarke, F.B.H.S.; W. Manning; Miss P. Manning, F.B.H.S.; W. Micklem, B.H.S.I.; Major Mortimer, B.H.S.I.; L. Sederholm; Mrs R. C. T. Sivewright, F.B.H.S. and R. C. L. Stillwell. The publishers wish to thank Brig. J. Grose, the original editor.

PART ONE

# Training the Rider

CHAPTER ONE

# The Position of the Rider

## INTRODUCTION

**1**  The basis of all equitation is the ability of the rider to sit in the saddle in the correct classical position and to be able to maintain this position without tension and under all circumstances. The word 'classical' is not used in a pedantic way but refers to a position which has become classical because it has evolved through the ages as the most practical way of riding a horse. Xenophon (430 to 354 BC) wrote of it; it is taught by the Spanish Riding School; and, subject to the certain modifications adopted by the Fédération Equestre Internationale, FEI, it is the basis of this book.

The aim is that a rider should place as much of his weight as possible where the horse can most easily carry it, that is, over the animal's centre of balance just behind the withers. By using an upright position the rider concentrates his point of balance so that horse and man share a common point of gravity and can work in harmony. Any deviation from this ideal position will be reflected in the horse's way of going and/or his temperament. It is, therefore, essential that every serious horseman works to achieve a truly classical seat until such a position becomes instinctive to him.

The above applies also to the classical jumping position, which is achieved by closing the angles of hip, knee and ankle joints, while remaining in balance with the horse.

## THE CLASSICAL OR BASIC POSITION

**2**  The position described in detail in paragraphs 3 and 4 below is that to be adopted for riding on the flat, including dressage. Besides being the one from which a rider can most easily influence his horse, it is also the most elegant. The rider sits square in the lowest part of the saddle, his weight equally distributed on his seat bones but with some weight absorbed by the thighs and the feet, the latter resting on the stirrups with only enough weight to keep the stirrups in place; the rider's point of balance is directly over that of the horse, i.e., behind the horse's withers. There must be no tension, physical or mental, if the correct position is to be achieved and maintained.

## OUTLINE FROM THE SIDE

**3** Viewed from the side, the correct outline is shown in fig. 1, with a vertical line running through the rider's ear, shoulder, hip and heel. This line remains unchanged except in the rising trot. The position of the body viewed from the side should be:

a  *Head:* The rider looks in the direction in which he is going, but if he needs to look down, he does so with the eyes only. The head should not be dropped nor poked forward and there must be no tension in the jaw.

b  *Shoulders:* Should be down and well back without being stiff. This is

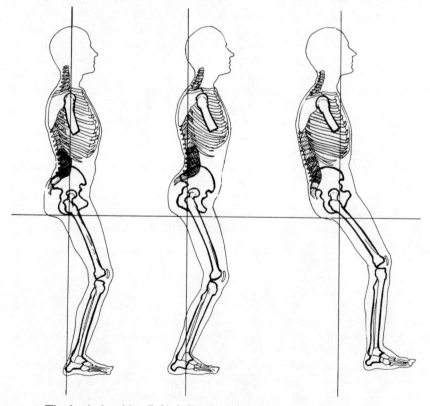

**1.** *The classical position (left), hollow back (centre) and collapsed seat (right).*

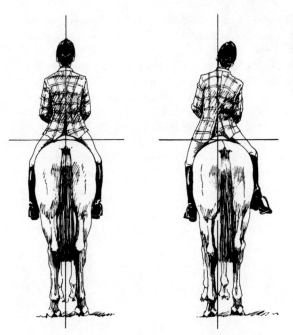

**2.** *The rider's position viewed from the rear. On the left (fig. 2a), the rider is sitting upright, but on the right (fig. 2b), he has collapsed his right hip.*

achieved by expanding the chest rather than squaring the shoulders.

c  *Back:* The body is upright, as in fig. 2, with the back straight but supple. It must not be hollowed nor rounded except to the extent that it follows the natural curvature of the spine.

d  *Waist:* Should not be allowed to collapse backwards (collapsed seat), forwards (hollow seat), or to one side (collapsed hip.) (*See* fig. 2.)

e  *Hip Joints:* These should be pressed slightly forward and the pelvis upright so that the side seams of the breeches are upright and at right angles to the horse's back.

f  *Legs:* The thigh should lie flat on the saddle and there should be no tension in the thigh, hip joint, or indeed anywhere in the legs. The knee points to the front, as does the toe, helping the rider to sit deeper in the saddle. The knee joint should not be forced into the saddle but be relaxed so that the lower leg hangs down, lying softly on the horse's side. The legs should be relaxed yet maintain a constant contact with the horse's sides.

g  *Feet:* The widest part of the foot rests on the stirrup iron with only sufficient weight to retain the irons. The stirrup irons should be level, with no extra weight on the inside or outside of the foot, the heel slightly lower than the toe with the ankle joint remaining supple.

h   *Arms and Hands:* The upper arm should be relaxed, hanging down, never behind the vertical. The shoulders and elbow joints should be flexible to allow the hands to follow the movements of the horse's head. There should be no tension in the forearm nor in the hand and there should be a straight line from the elbow, through the hands to the horse's mouth. Looking from above, the straight line will run from the outside of the forearm, through the back of the hand, down the rein, to the horse's mouth. The thumb should be uppermost. The reins are held at the base of the fingers and come out over the top of the hand, where the thumb rests lightly on them. The fingers should be closed but not clenched, so that if the rider were holding a bird in each hand, 'the bird would be allowed to breathe but not to fly away.'

*3. Viewed from above, the position of horse and rider on a straight line (left) and when turning to the right (right).*

## OUTLINE FROM THE REAR

**4** Viewed from the rear (*see* fig. 2) a straight line would run through the middle of the rider's head, down the spine, through the centre of the back of the saddle and the horse's spine. On turns and circles the angle of the rider's body should stay exactly in line with the angle of the horse's body. (*See* fig. 3.)

a   *Head:* The head and neck must be square on the shoulders and not tilted to either side.

b   *Shoulders:* The shoulders should be at equal height without hunching or stiffness.

c   *Elbows:* The elbows should be level with one another: not stretched away from the body nor glued to the sides, but hang naturally.

d   *Seat:* The hip joints should be square to the front with the weight resting evenly on the forward inner surface of both seat bones, the central seam of the breeches being in line with the centre of the saddle.

e   *Lower Legs:* The lower legs should be level with one another. They should hang down and not be stretched away from the horse's sides with the inside of the lower legs quietly in contact with the horse's sides.

f   *Feet:* The feet should have equal weight on both stirrup irons and look level without having more weight on the inside or outside of the irons. The ankles should be at equal angles.

## THE SEAT

**5** To use the seat correctly when riding it helps to understand its anatomy and methods of movement.

THE RELEVANT SECTORS ARE:

a   *the thighs:* (femurs) which at their upper ends form the balls of the ball and sockets of

b   *the hip joints:* The sockets of the right and left hip joints are about one third the way up the right and left

c   *hip bones:* (Each hip bone consists of the ilium above, the ischium below and behind, and the pubis below and in front. *See* fig. 4.) The two hip bones form the front, sides and part of the back of

d   *the pelvis:* an oval shaped (in horizontal section) almost rigid girdle. The lowest points of the pelvis are

e   *the seat bones:* The ridges of bone at the front of the pelvis which can be felt just below the waist are

f   *the crests of the ilium:* The lower forward points of the pelvis which can be felt at the bottom of the abdomen are the right and left

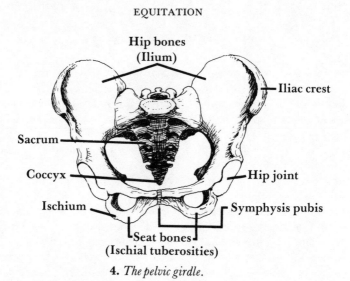

**Hip bones (Ilium)**

Iliac crest

Sacrum

Coccyx

Hip joint

Ischium

Symphysis pubis

Seat bones (Ischial tuberosities)

**4.** *The pelvic girdle.*

g  *pubic bones:* At the back the ring of the pelvic girdle is completed by
h  *the sacrum:* This consists of fused rigid vertebrae which articulate with
i  *the lumbar vertebrae:* which run from just above to just below the waist.
They are very mobile, and above them the thoracic vertebrae are more
rigid.

THE RIDER CAN MOVE HIS SEAT BECAUSE:

a  the lumbar spine is mobile.
b  the pelvis can be tipped. From the pivot of where the rigid sacrum (rear
section of the pelvis) and the mobile lumbar vertebrae are connected the
pelvis can be tipped forwards (crests of ilium forward, pubic bones
backward), and backwards largely through use of the abdominal and
back muscles.
c  the hip joints are mobile.

THE PELVIS CAN ALSO BE:

a  tipped sideways (by bending the lumbar vertebrae) when one hip joint
is lowered and moves sideways to result in a collapsed hip. (*See* paragraph 3d.)
b  turned in relation to the trunk to result in one seat bone moving forward
and the other backward.

*The hips.* The term tends to be used loosely and may refer to the hip joints or
the crests of the ilium or the ischium, ilium and pubis. In this book the latter
term is used, as this is the medical definition; but because this is a large area,
and because of the confusions over the word, more precise terminology, i.e.,
hip joint is preferred.

## POSITION IN MOVEMENT ON THE FLAT

**6**a *Walk:* The horse walks in four time. He nods his head as each foreleg comes to the ground, and to keep a constant rein contact, the rider's hands must go with this movement and not restrict it in any way. The fingers remain closed on the reins and the contact stays unaltered. The rider remains sitting upright, but his supple seat moves to allow and not restrict the horse's body movements. When the horse walks well there is considerable movement of his back muscles. This movement is essential if the horse is to remain supple, co-ordinated and free in his paces. Therefore, the rider must allow this movement to occur through supple action of his lower, but not upper back. It is usual for the pelvis to tip in the rhythm of the pace. A good exercise both for developing suppleness and feel is to allow the seat bones to move alternately so that as the left hindleg is lifted forward the rider allows his left seat bone forward in accordance with the horse's muscle movement and then the right seat bone with the right hindleg. This movement in the rider's seat should not be exaggerated and therefore barely perceptible to an on-looker.

b *Rising Trot:* The horse trots in two time. The rider rises on one beat of the trot and sits on the next; it is essential that this is done in perfect balance so as not to upset the horse's rhythm. The rider's body is inclined slightly forward from the pelvis with the pelvis tipped forward and he should sit softly without allowing the weight to go backwards. The shoulders and elbows allow the hands to go with the movement of the horse's head and neck, which in the trot hardly move.

c *Sitting Trot:* The rider does not rise but remains sitting with his seat bones in contact with the saddle. The body remains upright. The movement of the horse's back is absorbed mostly through the rider's seat but also through the knees and ankles, the hands keeping the consistent contact as in the rising trot. The spring of the trot is such that in absorbing the movement the rider should feel it rather like riding the crests of small waves. Thus, the thighs feel as if they are loose in their sockets and the pelvis tips forwards and backwards. As in the walk, this movement must not be exaggerated, to result in the back hollowing or the waist collapsing. Any tenseness or gripping will cause the rider to bump instead of remaining in a quiet balanced position in contact with the horse's back.

d *Canter:* The horse canters in three time. In the canter, the level of the horse's body alters from front to back. (*See* Part Two, Chapter 1 [10h].) The rider must therefore adjust to this alteration in the levelness of the horse as well as absorb the upward and downward spring. The rider must absorb the bounding movement of the canter with his seat and not by swinging his upper body backwards and forwards – which is a very common fault. The hip joints need to be pressed forward, the shoulders remaining on the vertical (not forward) and square to the horse's shoulders. The pelvis tips to follow the undulating movement of the canter. The three hoof beats should be felt and the rider's hip joint corresponding to the leading leg should be pressed slightly more forward than the other, i.e., if the near is leading then the left seat bone should be forward. The rider's legs must remain long, with the inside leg beside the girth and the outside slightly further behind. There must be no drawing up of either leg.

The horse moves his head up and down in time with the leading leg and, to retain a consistent rein contact, the hands must allow this, as they do in the case of the walk.

## THE JUMPING POSITION

7 When jumping, or indeed, when galloping on the flat, the rider must modify the Basic Seat, described above, partly to maintain his balance but also to take his weight off the horse's back.

TO ADOPT THE JUMPING POSITION THE RIDER:

a   shortens his stirrup leathers (the length depending on the work to be carried out), which closes the angles of the hips-knees-ankles,
b   inclines his body forward from the pelvis (the seat may be kept in light contact with the saddle or not, as desired),
c   increases the weight on the thigh, knee and stirrup,
d   he may turn his toes slightly out so as to tighten the leg muscles.
   The rider remains looking forward and with the back flat.

The hands stay well in front of the rider, in a straight line from the elbow through the forearm, hands and rein to the mouth, although the elbows may leave the sides.

The result is that the rider's weight is taken off the horse's back and the rider is able to stay in balance when travelling at speed.

## FAST WORK

8 In fast work on the flat the rider must take care that:
a   The stirrups are short enough otherwise the rider tends to stand in his

stirrups and open the angle of the knee. The result of this is that the seat bones are not close enough to the saddle.

b   The rider's body is not too far forward, i.e., the angle is not more than 45° from the vertical.

c   The reins are not too long with the rider's hands insufficiently advanced.

## THE POSITION IN MOVEMENT WHEN JUMPING
### (SEE FIG. 5.)

**9**  The position described in paragraph 6 above is the one generally taught to riders learning to jump. The rider's position in the various stages of jumping a fence are

a   *The Approach:* The approach is made in the basic jumping position described above, making sure that the angle of the body is not more than approximately 45° in front of the vertical. The seat bones may be just clear of, brushing, or lowered into, the saddle. Care must be taken not to get in front of or behind the movement when riding the last stride, but to stay in balance. This is particularly important with young or green horses.

**5.** *Positions from the stride before take off, to the landing.*

b *The Take-Off:* Depending on the size of the fence, the angle of the rider's body to the horse is closed, bringing the chest nearer to the mane. This must not be overdone nor must the angle of the knee be opened excessively. The knee must always be forward, pointed and deep in the saddle. The contact is lightened and the hands follow the movement of the horse's head and neck. The lower leg should remain in position during this phase and throughout the jump.

c *In Mid-Air:* Over the top of the fence the rider maintains this position.

d *The Descent:* On the descent the body remains inclined forward, and although the seat bones may brush the saddle, there should be no weight on them.

e *The Landing:* The rider resumes the original position, the stride after landing.

## AN ALTERNATIVE JUMPING POSITION

**10** Many riders, including experienced show jumpers and event riders, use a modified jumping seat, adapted from that described in paragraphs 7, 8 and 9 above. It is stressed that the difference between the two positions is one of degree and experienced riders should be able to adapt their position between the two as necessary.

In the alternative position, the stirrup leathers are longer, the amount varying according to the rider's conformation and suppleness. The seat bones rest on the saddle but the main weight is borne by the inside of the thigh and knee.

The body is upright, or nearly upright, but not behind the vertical.

The hands are well in front of the rider, with the elbows slightly in front of the top of the hips (the crests of the iliums). There is a straight line from the elbow, through the forearm, hand and rein, to the mouth.

THE POSITION AT THE VARIOUS STAGES OF A JUMP ARE:

a *The Approach:* The approach is made in the above position. The contact is kept the same throughout the approach.

b *The Take-Off:* The angle of the hip joint is closed, bringing the chest nearer to the horse's mane.

The weight is taken off the seat bones although the breeches may still brush the saddle, depending on the size of the fence.

The contact is lightened and the hands follow the movement of the horse's head and neck.

c *In Mid-Air:* Over the top of the fence the rider stays forward until the horse starts the descent. Over a wide fence this will be for a longer period than over an upright fence.

d  *The Descent and Landing:* The body on descent becomes more nearly upright and, on landing, resumes the approach position, the lower leg remaining in the correct position throughout the process of the jump.

## COMPARISON OF THE TWO JUMPING POSITIONS

**11** The advantages claimed for the modified jumping position are that it enables the rider to control his horse's impulsion and stride better when coming into a fence and on landing. Horses that are lazy or likely to refuse may be more easily controlled from this position. On the other hand, it requires considerably more agility on the rider's part if he is not to be left behind the movement with possible damage to the horse's back. Even when using the 'alternative' position, it is often advisable to 'ride in' in the basic position, especially on a young horse, as it takes the weight off the horse's back.

# CHAPTER TWO

# Establishing the Basic Position on the Lunge

## INTRODUCTION

**1** One of the best ways of establishing the correct position in the saddle and improving a rider's balance is for him to ride without stirrups both on and off the lunge. The main advantage of riding on the lunge is that the rider can leave the control of his horse to another and concentrate on his position, but he will only do this and ride without tension if he has complete confidence in the person doing the lungeing and if the horse is suitable.

This chapter is limited to giving guidance on how to establish a rider's basic position by riding on the lunge without stirrups. The technique of lungeing a horse, without a rider, differs considerably and is dealt with in Part Two, Chapter 21, which also covers the facilities and tack required for lungeing in more detail.

There will come a time when the novice rider will wish to dispense with the lunge and start riding, using reins and stirrups, and controlling his horse. This is acceptable, once the rider has acquired a stable seat, and is the next step in his education. The means by which control is exercised are discussed in Chapters 3 and 4.

Even after the lunge has been dispensed with and the rider controls his own horse, riding without stirrups is still a most useful way of developing the correct position in the saddle. Many advanced riders do much work without stirrups finding that they are more in harmony with their horse and so more effective.

## RESPONSIBILITIES OF AN INSTRUCTOR

**2** **Instructing the Rider**: Anyone undertaking the lungeing of a rider should not only be well versed in lungeing, but also sufficiently knowledgeable to be able to correct the rider's position and help him to maintain it at all paces; the instructor is responsible for modifying the horse's paces and transitions to suit the rider. Sometimes he may use an assistant to lead the horse and give confidence to or to support a novice in the first stages of riding on the lunge.

**3  The Rider's Safety**: When lungeing a rider, the instructor is entirely responsible for his safety and must do everything possible to avoid anything untoward happening which will reduce the rider's confidence. Only if a rider can work without tension will work on the lunge be of value. An instructor should pay attention to the following points, all of which have a bearing on the horse's and rider's safety:

a  Lungeing should be carried out in a satisfactory environment. (*See* paragraph 4 below.)

b  Tack should be strong and well fitted (paragraph 5 below).

c  The lunge horse should be suitable (paragraph 6 below).

d  Lessons should not be too long and must contain sufficient rest periods.

e  Instructor, rider and horse should be correctly turned out.

The instructor should always wear gloves when handling a lungeing rein and discard his spurs. The rider should wear breeches and boots or jodhpurs and must wear a hard hat.

## FACILITIES NEEDED

**4  The lungeing area**: Lungeing should always be carried out in a reasonably quiet place so that neither the horse's nor the rider's attention is distracted and the instructor's commands can be clearly heard by both. The going must be good and the whole area should be level and, if possible, be enclosed as this will greatly increase a novice rider's confidence and help the horse's concentration. It follows that an indoor riding school is often an ideal site for a lesson but it is certainly not essential, and, in any case, lungeing should not be carried out day after day, in the same place or the horse will become bored.

**5  Tack**: The tack needed when lungeing a horse and rider consists of

a  *A snaffle bridle:* if the reins are not removed, they should be twisted around under the neck and the throat strap put through one of the loops (*see* Part Two fig. 17) and not fixed to the saddle. If lungeing is being carried out in the open it is safer to knot the reins on the horse's neck so that the rider can pick them up in an emergency.

b  *A cavesson:* This is fitted over the bridle and buckled under the chin like a dropped noseband, or above the bit like a cavesson noseband, with the lunge rein fastened to the central swivel ring on the noseband. The noseband and cheek strap must be tightened sufficiently to avoid them pulling round or rubbing the horse's outside eye.

c  *A Lunge Rein:* Is about 10 metres (33 ft) long, made of linen webbing or nylon, with a large loop at one end and a swivel joint, attached to a buckle or spring clip, at the other.

d   *Side-Reins:* These are about 2 metres (6 ft) long and must be used with caution, only being fastened to the bit just before the horse starts to work on the lunge. They should run, horizontally, about half way up the horse's sides in straight lines from girth to mouth. When not in use they should be clipped to the D's of the saddle.

e   *A Saddle:* It is important that the saddle fits both horse and rider and the use of a numnah is recommended.

f   *A Lunge Whip*

g   *Brushing boots for all four legs*

**6   The Lunge Horse**: Ideally, the horse to be used by a rider on the lunge should be a specialist at the job, but a lunge horse must do other work if he is not to become thoroughly stale. Temperament is very important and he must be obedient to the human voice since, on the lunge, this will be the principle aid; the paces should be comfortable. Circling is a strain on a horse and a fit and mature animal of six or over should be used and the time spent on the lunge should not exceed twenty minutes (excluding rest periods) if the horse is being used actively.

## TECHNIQUE FOR LUNGEING A RIDER

**7   The Instructor**: The instructor should stand in the centre of the lungeing circle, which is normally about 10 metres (33 ft), or slightly less, in radius and drives the horse round him, holding the lunge rein in the hand to which the horse is moving, and holding the whip in his other hand. Instructors can hold the loop at the end of the lunge rein in either hand. The trainer must concentrate on the rider and on the horse's hind quarters rather than his forehand. It is important that the horse should describe a true circle and to ensure this the trainer should stand on one spot. A trained lunge horse should be obedient to the instructor's voice and the lunge whip should seldom have to be used, but when it is needed the horse should be lightly touched just above the hind fetlocks. Whenever the instructor moves closer to the horse, the whip is reversed, with the thong trailing to his rear.

**8   Length of a Lungeing Lesson**: As stated in paragraph 6 above, a horse being used actively should not be lunged for more than some twenty minutes, excluding rest periods. With a novice rider, however, where the horse will probably not be required to move so energetically, a half hour period, again excluding rest periods, is acceptable. Frequent rest periods will be needed since riding without stirrups can be tiring for riders. The horse should be worked equally on each rein.

**9    Preliminary Work**: Before the start of a lesson, an instructor will often wish to begin by lungeing the horse, without a rider, to settle him down; many riders like to 'warm up' by riding on the lunge but using their stirrups. Both measures may be used with advantage.

**10    Adopting the Classical Position**: The person lungeing and instructing must ensure that the rider takes up and maintains the correct position in the saddle as defined in Chapter 1. The rider, with the horse stationary, places himself in the deepest part of the saddle, with his weight on his seat bones and his legs hanging loosely down against the saddle. To achieve this position, he should take hold of the front of his saddle with both hands and gently pull his seat into the lowest part, making himself as tall and upright as possible so that a vertical line running from his ear through the point of his shoulder, bisects his hip joint and touches the back of the heel. The side reins should not be attached at this stage.

The following two points should be particularly noted:

a    That there is no deviation from the line, ear – shoulder – hip joint, although later the heel can come forward of this line without ill effect in the training of horses. A rider sitting on his fork will tend to be in front of the line and if he transfers his weight from his seat bones to his buttocks the tendency will be for him to be behind the line. (*See* figs. 1 and 6.)

b    That the inner thigh muscles are relaxed so that the knee lies sufficiently low on the saddle to adopt the correct position.

**11    To assist in achieving the correct position:** The following simple and short exercise may be carried out before starting work, either when halted or at a walk. The movements should never be jerky and the timing must be left to the rider, the exercise being repeated two or three times.

The rider, holding the front of the saddle, stretches both legs sideways away from the horse's side. He then allows the legs to relax completely and fall gently back onto the saddle, the knee being as low as possible, without straining.

**12    To build up confidence:** At all three paces and on both reins, the rider can take the inside hand off the saddle and to allow the arm to hang down just behind his thigh for a circle or two. The whole arm should be relaxed as this exercise should begin to instil in the rider the importance of a relaxed upper arm once he is holding the reins. The rider should refrain from holding the saddle with the inside hand alone as this may result in some loss of balance and a tendency to lean into the circle. However, once he can let go of the saddle, both arms may be dropped together, care being taken that the waist does not collapse or the shoulders become rounded.

**13   Work at the walk**: Lungeing the rider at the walk has little value except to give confidence to beginners or nervous riders. There is very little upward thrust in the movement of the horse's back but an active walk will displace the rider's balance on a horizontal and slightly diagonal plane and riders must be taught that this motion must be absorbed through the suppleness of their seat and not result in a rocking action of the upper body. (*See* Chapter 1, paragraph 6a.)

Although all exercises that follow can be carried out at the walk, for more experienced riders the walk is best used for checking the rider's position and during rest periods when the rider is allowed to sit at ease.

**14   Sitting to the trot**: Once in the correct position at the walk and with the rider still holding the saddle if required, the horse can be sent quietly forward into a trot, as long as the speed, action and spring of it is well within the rider's capabilities. Advanced riders will instinctively try to influence this. They should normally not do so, but accept what the horse offers and concentrate on maintaining their own position without gripping or tension. Only when the seat and balance are fully established should the seat be used to control the movement and action of the horse. At the sitting trot, the rider should adjust to the two-time rhythm of the trot and, remaining supple and without tension, allow the weight of the body to sink softly down into the saddle as each pair of diagonal legs meet the ground; horse and rider will then rebound as one during the periods of suspension. Once the rider has achieved this, he will be able to sit still in relation to the movement of his horse. (*See* Chapter 1, paragraph 6.)

**15   Rising to the trot**: Rising to the trot without stirrups has little to commend it, except as a strengthening exercise for jumping and racing. Should a rider need to improve his technique the stirrups should therefore be re-attached and the leathers so adjusted that he can make and easily retain contact, with the widest part of his foot on the iron and with the heel lower than the toe. It is important that the length of leather is adapted to suit the rider's position and not the other way round. If the leathers are too short either tension will develop, especially in the knees and ankles, or more likely, the rider will move his seat back in the saddle. If too long the rider will constantly be dropping his toes to make contact with the irons and so weakening his whole position.

Once the stirrups are the correct length and the horse is moving in a soft, springy trot the rider should allow this action gently to lift his seat bones from the saddle on every other diagonal stride. To compensate for this movement the body should also go slightly forward from the top of the hips. (*See* Chapter 1, paragraph 6.) Retaining this position the rider then sinks softly back into the saddle on the next stride. The feeling should be of 'going forward and down and not up in the air and back' (de Nemethy). The whole movement should be initiated by the action of the horse and not by the rider.

**16  Changing the diagonal**: When rising to the trot on the lunge the rider should rise in time with and as the horse's outside shoulder goes forward, thus returning to the saddle as that leg and the inside hindleg hit the ground. This is known as rising on, or using, the outside diagonal which not only makes it easier for the horse to maintain his balance on the circle but prevents one sided muscular development. It also has an important part to play in the use of the aids once the horse is off the lunge. Riders should be encouraged constantly to change the diagonal by sitting down for one additional stride before rising again until they can tell instinctively which diagonal they are using.

**17  Work at the canter**: The difficulties entailed when riding at a canter on the lunge are greater than at the walk or trot and this should never be attempted without an experienced person in charge and in a quiet situation away from other horses.

Centrifugal force is more noticeable at this pace and riders should guard against the use of grip to maintain their position. Nor should the upper body rock in rhythm with the changing horizontal levels of the horse's back; this should be absorbed through supple seat. (*See* Chapter 1, paragraph 6.) Not all exercises can be carried out at the canter and the suitable ones are mentioned in the following paragraphs.

## EXERCISES

**18  General**: When a rider has the confidence and ability to let go of the saddle and ride easily while maintaining his position without gripping, for about five minutes on each rein, further mounted exercises should be attempted. These are designed to improve the rider's position, suppleness and balance and, in the case of the novice, to increase his confidence.

The following general points apply to all exercises on the lunge whether at the walk, trot or canter, and should be observed by the rider and the person lungeing him or supervising the exercise:

a  As the basis of riding is rhythm, all exercises should be carried out rhythmically in time with the horse.

b  The exercises should develop balance, suppleness and strength without producing tension anywhere.

c  The movement of one part of the body should not be reflected in another part.

d  Breathing should be deep and controlled with a slight emphasis on exhalation, as this helps relaxation. No exercise in the saddle should make the pupil out of breath.

e  All exercises should be carried out on both reins. Few riders sit in an identical position on each side and most have a tendency to twist in the saddle, causing one leg to move forward and the other slightly back.

f  Twenty minutes excluding rest periods, should be the maximum for work on the lunge for any but the most experienced riders.

**19**  The following exercises are suitable for riders on the lunge:

a  *Correcting the position.* The object is to develop a sense of balance and timing:

    I  The horse is made to perform transitions from walk to trot, trot to walk.

    II  The rider holds the front of his saddle, straightens his body upwards at the same time as pulling gently down into the saddle and stretching down with both legs, i.e., there should be an upward and downward correction. This should be done immediately prior to transitions and is a useful exercise at other times. Later the muscle influence of these movements is used to warn the horse that something is about to be asked of him and to ensure the rider is in the correct position to apply the aids. The rider should develop the habit of correcting his position prior to asking anything of the horse.

    III  As the rider progresses, the same exercise may be carried out with the hands in the rein position, i.e., holding imaginary reins, great care being taken that the correct position is not lost, particularly during transitions.

    IV  Advanced riders can carry out this exercise in the walk, trot and canter, and include direct transitions to the halt. In this case, if the instructor and the horse are sufficiently expert, such transitions may be done without voice aids to prevent pre-warning the rider.

b  *Shoulder Exercise:* In shoulder shrugging the object is to remove any tension from the shoulders and the base of the neck. Both shoulders are drawn up as high as possible towards the ears (taking care not to tilt the head back or stick the elbows out), and then allowed to drop back into place. They must not be lowered hesitantly or be pulled down forcibly. This should be repeated five or six times; it must be done in an easy rhythm and without setting up any tension in the back or arms.

c *Head and Neck Exercises:* The object is to rid the neck and jaw of tension. These exercises are a logical follow-on to the previous one.

  I The head is allowed to turn steadily anti-clockwise and then clockwise. Care should be taken that the head does not tilt.

  II Without raising the chin the head is rolled steadily first to one side and then the other, with the ear as nearly as possible resting on the shoulders, which must not be allowed to lift.

  III The head is allowed to roll steadily forward until the chin is resting on the chest. Care should be taken that the back does not become rounded.

**N.B.** I) and III) should be performed at the halt only.

d *Arm and Shoulder Exercises:* The object is to flatten and stretch the muscles of the abdomen and free the shoulder joints.

  I Steadily raise alternate arms with fingers stretched and the elbow joint straight until it reaches maximum height with the elbow joint beside the ear, palm facing forward.

  II Circle the arms slowly to the rear three or four times before returning to normal position. The exercise may then be carried out with both arms simultaneously. The swing should always be backwards and in rhythm with the horse's stride. No force should be used or effort made to complete a full backward circle.

  III Instead of circling the arms backwards, they may be moved backwards as far as they will go without strain and keeping the arm and fingers straight. The arm is then returned to the vertical position. In both II) and III) the shoulder and hip joints must remain parallel.

  IV Raise the arms so that they are horizontal. Turn the body from the waist alternatively to the left and the right, while maintaining the arms on the horizontal and at 180° to each other. The seat must remain still. This can be done at the walk and trot.

e *Spine and Hip Joints:* The object of these exercises is to make the spine and hip joints supple.

  I *Arm Turning:* Allow the arms to hang limply down and place one hand on the horse's withers and the other over the back of the saddle. Change position by twisting from the waist without losing correct position or the rhythm of the pace. The seat must not move in the saddle nor the backward arm be taken beyond the line of the horse's spine. This exercise may be safely carried out at the halt, walk or trot, but the pupil should be fairly competent before attempting it at the canter.

  II *Jockey Position:* While holding the front of the saddle, draw legs up closing the angles of the ankles, knees and hips and come forward with the body into the racing position. Maintain position for a few strides at first, but gradually hold for longer and longer. This can be done at the walk and trot.

    III  *Scissors:* Straighten legs and while maintaining seat bones in the saddle swing alternately one leg back and the other forwards. This can be done at the walk and trot.

    IV  *Touching Toes:* Raise one hand and lower to touch toe on opposite side. Repeat with other hand. This can be done at all paces.

f    *Ankle Exercise:* Turn ankles in as full a circle as possible, firstly clockwise and then anti-clockwise. This can be done at all paces.

**20   Value of Lungeing**:

a   It is one of the best ways of establishing the correct position and this is important for three reasons: firstly, to balance the load the horse is asked to carry; secondly, to enable the rider to apply the aids quietly and effectively; and, thirdly, to enable the rider to look as elegant as possible.

b   Helps to make rider supple and therefore more able to follow the movements of the horse.


# FITNESS OF THE RIDER

**21**  Every rider must be reasonably fit if he is to be able to maintain the correct position in the saddle, assist his horse and enjoy his riding. It is a surprising fact that the energy consumed in riding is of the same order as that used in such obviously physically demanding sports as running or cycling, so that even a novice requires a degree of basic fitness. For the advanced and for the competitive rider, such as the jockey, three-day eventer, show jumper or dressage rider, a much higher standard of physical fitness is needed.

**22**  **Methods of Achieving Fitness**: While daily riding is in itself a good way of keeping fit, it is certainly not enough to reach the standard of fitness required for competition. For this, the rider's heart and lungs must work efficiently, the muscles of the back and leg should be in particularly good condition. He must be supple in his body and excess fat must be avoided.

    It is generally agreed that the best way to keep fit is to run regularly, although skipping, swimming and cycling, are all useful aids to fitness. There are also many more mounted exercises which are suitable for riders of all stages, and of course, dismounted exercises and yoga, which help promote suppleness and co-ordination. Among the many books on the subject of physical fitness, *New Aerobics* by Kenneth H. Cooper, which is available in paperback, is one that is recommended.

It is most important not to overdo physical training, which should always be progressive and take into account the rider's age and medical condition. In special cases, medical advice should be sought before a strenuous course of training is undertaken.

CHAPTER THREE

# The Theory of the Aids

## INTRODUCTION

**1**  Aids are the language of horsemanship and, like all languages, have a basic structure, but it is emphasis and timing which lend them expression and refinement.

It is essential that anyone who wishes to ride well should understand the use, the reasons for and the effect of the aids, before he tries to teach them to his horse. The horse must be taught stage by stage and with complete clarity until the rapport between rider and horse is built up to such a level that it appears that the rider has but to think for the horse to obey willingly. This is the essence of true horsemanship. A trainer who can combine intelligence with mental and physical control and co-ordination can produce a highly trained, alert and happy horse, working with ease and complete confidence in his rider.

## DEFINITION AND TYPES OF AIDS

**2**  An aid is the signal or means by which a rider conveys his wishes to his horse. It refers to any action by the rider which results in physical or mental communication between him and his horse.

Aids are sub-divided into natural and artificial as follows:
a   *Natural Aids:* The rider's voice, legs, seat and hands.
b   *Artificial Aids:* Whips, spurs and any form of strap (other than the reins) which control or position the horse, with or without the rider's help. Examples are, standing or running martingales, draw or running reins. Only the whip and spur have a place in classical equitation and are the only artificial aids considered in this chapter.

## THE VOICE

**3**  The voice by its tone can encourage, correct, sooth or reward. It is also used to give commands, particularly on the lunge and with a young horse

30

when it is first ridden. The horse learns that sharp quick commands 'walk on', 'trot', 'canter' mean to go forward, and low and drawn-out 'woaah', 'waalk', 'trrot' to reduce the pace.

## THE LEGS

4   The major influences are to:
a   Create forward movement.
b   Activate the hindquarters.
c   When used independently, indicate direction.

5   **Identical Use of the Legs**: The effect of using both legs by the girth is to encourage the horse to move forward. When first handled, any horse will react to human contact by withdrawing from it. As flight is their natural defence, when first mounted and feeling the legs of the rider enclosing its rib cage, the reaction is to move forward away from the pressure. This is the basis of all training and is developed and refined by constant repetition, until the slightest pressure with the inside of the rider's leg will result in the horse moving forward.

6   **Individual use of the Legs**: Once this reaction of moving forward is established the application of either of the rider's legs by the girth will encourage the horse to move the hind leg on that side forward. Since it will also be instinctive for the horse to try to evade the pressure on the ribs it will also tend to bring the leg forward and slightly under the weight of the body preparatory to turning the hindquarters away from the point of stimulus. This effect is used to move the horse laterally (sideways), but if this is not desired, and the horse simply required to turn a corner, then the rider prevents the hindquarters turning by placing his other leg slightly further back from the girth. Hence, while both legs cause the horse to go forward, the rider's inside leg by the girth accentuates the forward movement while the outside leg, slightly behind the girth controls the hindquarters.

7   **Response to the Leg Aids**: The leg aids are most effective when
a   Applied with vibrant changing pressure and not a constant squeeze.
b   Not used in time with the horse's stride as the constant rhythm has a soporific effect.
c   Applied as lightly as possible, since heavy thumping with the legs, heels and spurs, will cause the horse to become dead to the leg and to draw back rather than go freely forward.
**N.B.** A horse which reacts to leg aids by drawing back is said to be 'behind

the leg', and a horse that goes freely forward at the slightest indication from the rider's legs is said to be 'in front of the leg'.

*When the horse responds* to the leg aids, the rider's legs should return to their normal position, resting at the horse's side until pressure has to be re-applied to maintain impulsion and straightness or to increase or change the pace.

## THE SEAT

**8** The major influences are on:
a Impulsion,
b Outline,
c Direction.

**9** **Use of the Seat Aids**: The seat aids can be used beneficially only if the rider has an independent seat. The novice rider should concentrate on using his seat only insofar as he allows the horse's movement to go 'through', i.e., he allows the horse's back muscles to operate freely so that the actions of the hindquarters and forehand are co-ordinated and not separated by a stiff back. The rider must allow the horse to remain supple and swing his back. Thus the rider should not sit heavily and stiffly to suppress the movement 'through' the horse's back and to make the outline hollow; but as described in Chapter 1, paragraph 6a, c, and d. A rider can start to use the seat aids when he is supple enough in his seat to allow the horse to move through his back, when he can feel the actions of the hind legs and his seat is indepen-dent enough to be able to apply an aid without setting up undesired changes or movements elsewhere in his body.

**10** *The seat aids are applied* by the rider controlling the actions of his hip joints and pelvis rather than allowing them to move freely in accordance with the horse's back movements. This is achieved by:
a Sitting more deeply, lengthening the legs and deepening the knees, but not collapsing the body. The seat sinks softly down into the saddle in rhythm with the footfalls of the horse; both will rebound together, the spring of the pace should then be softer and higher and without interfer-ence to the horse's balance.
b Correcting the position. The rider takes a deep breath, correcting his body upwards and, at the same time, deepens his seat and lengthens his legs to correct his seat and legs downwards. (*See also* Chapter 2 [19a].)
c Altering the angle of the pelvis from its upright position to tip forward (as in rising trot and rein back) or backward when the seat bones and the hip joints will go forward. (Used in driving exercises.) (*See* fig. 6.)

*6. The driving seat. The pelvis has been tipped backward (seat bones forward). It is useful to compare this fig. 6 with fig. 1.*

d   Unilateral use of the seat when one hip/seat bone comes or is pushed further forward than the other to influence direction and/or position of the hind legs.

e   Transfer of a little weight from one seat bone to another. This helps the rider to influence the direction of the movement and the action of the hind legs. It is used particularly in lateral work. Until the rider however, has a strong and independent seat it is easy for a transfer of weight to produce bad side effects, such as collapsed hips, so weight aids should only be used by more experienced riders.

## THE HANDS

11   The major influences are to:

a   Contain the impulsion created by the rider's legs (and seat) in the hindquarters. (Impulsion is the energy created by the activity of the hindquarters.)

b   Control the speed.

c   Help to some extent the balance.

d   Indicate direction.

*The hands are only supplementary* and complementary to the seat and leg aids. Except for the very young horse the rider should apply the leg (and seat) aids before the hands otherwise the hindquarters will tend to fall out behind and the impulsion will be lost rather than contained.

**12   Response to hand aids**: Through the reins and the bit the hands are a telephone to the horse's brain and their use has a paramount effect on its mental and physical attitude. To be most effective the hands should:

a   Never pull backwards.

b   Remain still in relation to the movement of the horse and entirely independent of the action of any other part of the rider's body.

c   Maintain a consistent light sympathetic but elastic contact with the bit (except when riding on a loose rein). The horse loses his sense of security if the rein contact is inconsistent.

**13 Individual use of the hands**: The tension in the reins is not the same in both hands when working on turns or circles, at the canter, and when correcting the natural crookedness of the horse. It is only when working a straight horse on straight lines at the walk and trot that the rider can aim for an even feel in both hands. For most of the time the reins should be used as follows.

a   *Outside Hand:* The hand on the opposite side to the rider's inside leg will receive some of the impulsion sent forward from the horse's inside hind leg. To control this the rider maintains a positive contact with the horse, i.e., one that neither releases nor pulls back the rein but maintains a consistent sympathetic contact in relation to the movement and therefore goes with it.

b   *Inside Hand:* The inside hand accepts and guides the inside bend of the horse, a bend which is created by the rider's seat and leg aids. The contact should be light and flexible to encourage the relaxation of the horse's lower jaw and the acceptance of the bit.

The principle is that the outside hand maintains a positive contact which controls the pace and assists the balance, while the inside hand is more flexible and indicates the bend.

**14   Riding on a long and on a loose Rein**: A horse can be ridden on a long rein, but the rider should maintain impulsion with his legs and seat while allowing the horse to relax and to stretch forward and down with his head and neck and to lengthen his stride. The rider, by opening his fingers, lets the reins slide as the horse asks for the extra length but does not completely lose contact. This is often described as keeping contact 'by the weight of the reins alone'.

There are times when a horse is ridden on a loose rein without any contact at all. A free walk, or walk on a loose rein, is ridden in the same way as a walk on a long rein, but all contact with the horse's mouth is abandoned and the horse is kept straight by the use of the rider's seat and legs alone. This is a pace of rest.

Work on a long and loose rein may be used at all three paces providing impulsion and balance are maintained.

**15  Methods of Holding the Reins**: There are many different but acceptable methods of holding the reins; some of the main ones are mentioned and illustrated in figs 7a, b, c and d.

A            B

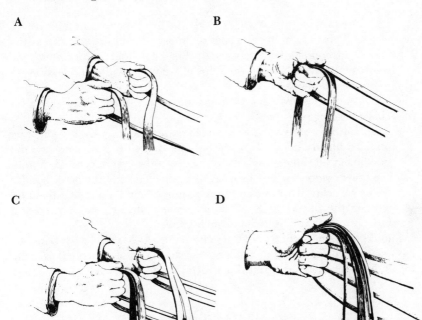

C            D

**7.** *Snaffle reins held in both hands (A), in one hand (B), double reins in both hands (C) and one hand (D).*

In most methods of holding the reins, the reins run from the horse's mouth, through the fingers, across the palm of the hand and out between the thumb and forefinger, with the thumb on top of the rein. The hand must be lightly closed (Chapter 1, páragraph 3h). In all cases it is the pressure of the thumbs on the reins over the forefingers which prevent the rein from slipping, and not the grip of a clenched hand or fingers.

a  *Snaffle Bridle:* When held in both hands, the reins pass between the third and fourth fingers, across the palm of the hand and out between the first finger and thumb; alternatively, the reins run round the outside of the little finger and out between the first finger and the thumb. When held in one hand, the most commonly used methods are to put the rein being moved between the thumb and first finger and out at the bottom of the hand, or to put it between the second or third finger and out between the first finger and thumb.

b  *Double Bridle:* When held in both hands, three recommended methods are

I  The bridoon rein passes outside the little finger, and the curb, or bit rein, between the third and little finger; the rein passes across the palm of the hand and out between the first finger and thumb. This is the most usual way of holding the reins of a double bridle and less severe than other methods.

II  As in (1) above, except that the position of the bridoon and bit reins are reversed.

III  Both bit reins are held in one hand separated by the second or by the third finger and the bridoon rein, on that side, passes outside the little finger; all three reins pass out between the first finger and thumb. The other bridoon rein is held between the fingers of the other hand.

The bit reins are adjusted to the required length on taking them up between the fingers and thereafter are not altered, the horse being ridden on the bridoon reins in each hand.

Should the rider wish to hold the reins in one hand, say, the left hand, he has only to transfer the right snaffle rein to the left hand, placing it over the top of the index finger and allowing the slack to hang down from the palm.

## THE ARTIFICIAL AIDS

**16  The whip**: The whip helps to reinforce the leg aids should they prove insufficient.

APPLICATION: It should be used behind the leg to emphasise the aid or to ask for more attention.

On occasion it will be necessary to change the hand in which the whip is held. To do this all the reins are put into the hand holding the whip and the free hand then takes hold of the whip below the holding hand, the back of the hand towards the rider's body. The whip is brought quietly across to the other side with the tapered end of the whip passing in front of the rider's face; the rein is then retaken by the whip hand. An alternative method is to put all the reins into the hand holding the whip; then the free hand takes hold of the whip above the holding hand, and draws it through the hand. The whip is then brought quietly across to the other side, tapered end downwards. The reins are then picked up again.

The schooling whip is used for schooling on the flat. It should be between 0.90 metres (3 ft) and 1.2 metres (4 ft) so that it is long enough to apply without taking the hand off the rein. The wrist is flicked to result in a tickle or a tap whenever required, behind the saddle.

The shorter whip, used for jumping, must not exceed 75 cms (30 ins). The whip hand should be taken off the rein and both reins held in one hand and the whip applied behind the saddle. The rider should practice this action and the ability to change whip hands.

**17   The spurs**: Like the whip the spurs help to reinforce the leg aids should they prove insufficient. They should allow greater stillness in the rider's position and when using the aids.

APPLICATION: When used, the spurs should only brush the skin. Spurs are a refinement of the aids and should not be used as a sole means of creating impulsion. Consequently, the rider must be able to apply his legs without the spurs touching the horse.

Spurs are rarely used in the early training of a horse and are not suitable for use by inexpert horsemen.

The artificial aids are only brought into action if the legs are not effective.

## COMBINED USE OF AIDS

**18**   Although every aid is considered separately above, they are always used in relation to each other. For example, the rider must first create the impulsion with his legs and seat before attempting to control it with his hands, and never the other way round.

## SUMMARY

**19**   Good aids are those which:
a   Are effective without causing noticeable movement in the rider or difficulties for his mount.

b   Enable the rider to maintain his seat and balance without dependence on the reins.
c   Ensure that the forward impetus of the horse is given willingly and completely into the rider's control.
d   Dictate the pace and/or the direction of the movement.

**20** *Aids are misused* if they:
a   Position or restrain the horse's body or speed by force.
b   Create more impulsion than the pace demands.
c   Fail to create enough impulsion to cause the horse to keep accepting the bit.
d   Fail to allow the rider's weight to move in harmony with that of the horse.
e   Fail to allow the hands to follow the horse's movement.
f   Are neither definite nor sufficiently clear for the horse to comprehend their meaning.
g   Are used involuntarily and without reason or anticipation.
h   Are used roughly, obviously, or to punish without justification.

CHAPTER FOUR

# The Use of the Aids

## INTRODUCTION

**1**  This chapter describes how the rider uses the aids to convey his wishes to his horse. The aids are comparatively few but the way they are applied, for example, the degree of pressure of each leg and of contact in each rein, can vary greatly and their use calls for skill and tact on the part of the rider.

For the aids to be most effective the rider must be in balance himself, and this is best achieved by establishing the classical position.

**2**  **Definitions**: For fuller definitions of the movements refer to the British Horse Society's Rules for Dressage, and the Fédération Equestre Internationale (FEI) Rules for Dressage Events.

The terms *'inside'* and *'outside'* are used frequently and refer to the slight curve throughout the length of the horse's body, 'inside' always being the concave side of the horse when correctly bent, and vice versa; they do not refer to the sides of the school or manege.

## FORWARD MOVEMENT

**3**  In all forward movement it is essential that the rider looks ahead to the point towards which he is asking the horse to move.

The first aid used by the rider is to activate the horse's hind legs into forward movement. To achieve this into the walk or trot (often referred to as 'moving off' or 'going forward into'); or into the canter (usually called 'striking off'), or for other upward transitions, the aids are as follows:

a  *Moving Off and Upward Transitions:* The rider

  i  Checks his position.

  ii  Maintains a light contact through the reins with the horse's mouth.

  iii  Applies extra pressure with both legs by the girth – not a steady squeeze but a series of quick, vibrant touches with the inside of his calf muscles.

  iv  Advanced riders who are able to feel the natural inclination of their horse to favour a left or right bend should compensate for this when moving off into a faster pace by adopting the opposite position, i.e., position right on a horse with a preference for a left bend. (*See* paragraph 10 below.) This helps maintain suppleness and keep the horse straight.

b *Striking Off:* The rider

   i   Checks his position.

   ii   Asks his horse for position right or left according to which leading leg is required. (*See* paragraphs 9 and 10 below.)

   iii   Applies the outside leg back behind the girth to encourage the horse's hind leg on that side to move forward and so start the sequence of the canter pace (Part Two, Chapter 1.9).

   iv   Applies the inside leg by the girth to encourage forward movement.

   v   Moves the inside seat bone forward, and when the canter is established, the weight comes slightly to that inner side.

c *Upward transitions within a pace:* For transitions between collected, working, medium, and extended paces, the rider

   i   Checks his position.

   ii   Increases the impulsion so that the steps become shorter and higher to make it easier for the horse to lengthen when asked. This is usually achieved through the half-halt. (*See* paragraph 7 below.)

   iii   Applies his legs by the girth and pushes his seat bones forward (tipping the pelvis backwards).

   iv   Maintains a supple seat, through movement of his hip joints and pelvis to allow the horse's back muscles to move freely and for its outline to remain rounded. At the trot it is often necessary to rise rather than sit to maintain the rounded outline.

## CONTROLLING THE FORWARD MOVEMENT

**4**   The reins are used to control the forward movement, but except in the case of a very young horse their action must be in conjunction with the legs (and seat) aids in order to keep the hindquarters engaged. These reins aids are applied through sympathetic movement of the fingers and the hands.

**5**   *Downward transitions:* The rider

a   Checks his position.

b   Creates a little more impulsion, usually through the half-halt.

c   Uses more and more restraining, but allowing, hands to accept and control this impulsion until the desired pace is established. These hand aids should be applied in co-ordination with tactful seat and leg aids so

that the hindquarters are engaged during the downward transition.
d  As soon as the new pace is established, rides forward with the seat and legs to maintain the rhythm.
e  Takes care that his balance is maintained so that he is not left forward of the movement.

**6  The Halt**: (Part Two, Chapter 4.35) The aids are the same as for all downward transitions, but in this case the restraining but allowing hands finally stop the movement. Even in the halt impulsion should not be allowed to escape, so the rider maintains a light contact with the bit and his legs remain on the horse's sides.

**7  The Half-Halt**: (Part Two, Chapter 4.36) This is a hardly visible moderated version of the halt. 'The momentary collection of a horse in motion' (Von Blixen-Finecke).
The rider:
a  Applies momentarily the driving aids of the seat and the legs.
b  Restrains momentarily with his hands the horse's consequent desire to go forward so that the horse becomes more collected, rather than going faster.
c  Releases momentarily the pressure on the reins before restoring the original contact.

**8  The Rein-Back:** (Part Two, Chapter 4.47)
The rider:
a  Establishes a square halt with the horse remaining on the bit.
b  Eases the weight in the saddle by tilting the pelvis forward, in order to discourage the horse from hollowing his back.
c  Applies the legs on the girth.
d  Prevents the consequent inclination to move forward by restraining aids on the reins.
e  Releases the pressure on the reins as soon as the horse steps back. It is vital that the rider does not pull backwards on the reins as the horse will then resist or run back stiffly. The horse must also be kept straight by appropriate use of the rider's legs and, if necessary, the reins.

## CHANGES OF DIRECTION
(SEE FIG. 3.)

**9**  To change direction the rider:
a  Checks his position.
b  Uses the outside rein to follow the movement of the horse's head and

neck with a constant contact, unless he brings it into use to control the impulsion and to some extent the balance.

c    Applies his fingers on the inside rein intermittently to establish a more flexible contact and a slight bend, and thus indicate direction.

d    Uses both legs and a supple seat to maintain impulsion, but the inside leg by the girth dominates and must be sufficiently effective to induce the horse to bring his hind leg, on that side, forward and slightly under the centre of his body; only then will the horse be able to follow the true line of the circle.

e    Rests his outside leg slightly further back, but not quite as far back as when asking for the canter. The leg remains in this position ready to be used if the horse's hindquarters start to swing to the outside of the circle.

f    Turns his shoulders to the inside, following those of the horse.

g    Transfers slightly more weight onto the inner seat bone while maintaining the correct upright position, and most riders bring their inner seat bone forward.

By using these aids much of the impulsion, produced by the rider's inside leg by the girth, will be transferred diagonally towards the outside shoulder, and is controlled by the rider's passive outside rein. The inside rein keeps the horse's mouth supple and indicates a slight bend to the inside.

**10    Position right and left**: A rider is said to be in position right and is

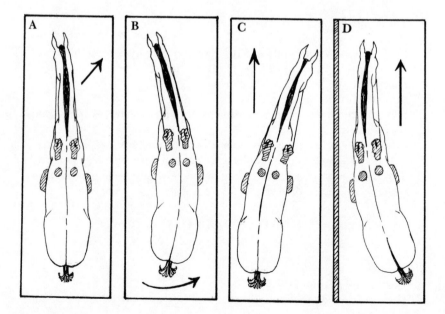

asking his horse to go in position right when he applies the above aids with his right leg as the inside leg, i.e., he is ready to turn right.

In position left, the left is the rider's inside leg.

The rider spends most of the time in position right or left because of the need to combat the horse's natural crookedness, the frequency of turns, the action of the horse at the canter and as a preparation for many movements.

## LATERAL WORK

**11** Lateral work refers to any form of movement wherein at least one of the horse's hind feet follow in a different track to that of the fore feet; the horse moving sideways as well as forwards.

**12 Leg Yielding**: (Part Two, Chapter 4.52) In the leg yield the horse is straight, except for a slight bend at the poll, allowing the rider to see the eyebrow and nostril on the inside. This bend is in the opposite direction to that which he is moving. The inside legs pass and cross the outside legs. (*See* fig. 8.)

This is the most basic of the lateral movements and can be carried out in working trot. Hence, many riders and/or horses start lateral work with this exercise.

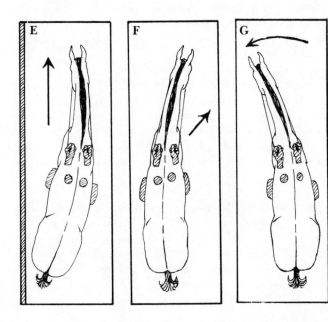

**8.** *Position of the horse, and the riders' seat bones, legs and hands in (A) Leg Yield, (B) Turn on the Forehand, (C) Shoulder In, (D) Travers, (E) Renvers, (F) Half Pass, (G) Pirouette.*

The rider:

a  Corrects his position.

b  Applies the inside leg by the girth. This is the dominant leg causing the horse not only to step forward but also to bring his inside leg further under his body and slightly in front of the other hind leg.

c  Keeps his outside leg just behind the girth and applies when necessary to keep the horse straight and/or to maintain the forward movement.

d  Asks with the inside rein for a slight bend at the poll so that the rider can see the eye and arch of the nostril.

e  Uses the outside rein to regulate the bend to help balance the horse and prevent the shoulder from falling out.

**13  The Turn on the Forehand:** (Part Two, Chapter 4.37) The horse's hindquarters rotate around the forehand; either away from the direction of the bend or, alternatively, in the direction of the bend. (*See* fig. 8.)
The rider:

a  Corrects his position.

b  Maintains the walk or halts momentarily.

c  Indicates the direction by asking for a slight bend to the inside.

d  Applies vibrant pressures with his inside leg on the girth.

e  At the time of c) brings the outside leg slightly further behind the girth, where it can be applied to contain the impulsion and control the movement if the horse starts to swing around too fast.

f  Uses the outside rein to restrain the forward movement.

g  The seat bones are turned so that they can remain central in the saddle and parallel to the horse's hips.

h  Upon completion the horse should go forward.

AN ALTERNATIVE: The turn on the forehand ridden in the above manner results in the horse moving his hindquarters away from the direction in which his body is bent. The turn on the forehand can also be executed by reversing the aids, when the rider's outside leg becomes the dominant one to cause the horse to step forward and in front of the inside hind leg as in travers (*see below*, paragraph 15); the horse then moves the hindquarters in the direction of the bend.

**14  The Shoulder-in:** (Part Two, Chapter 4.53) In the shoulder-in the horse moves at an angle of about 30° to the direction of the movement, with the whole horse bent slightly, but uniformly, from the poll to the tail around the rider's inside leg, while looking away from the direction in which he is moving. The horse's inside foreleg passes and crosses in front of the outside leg; the inside hind leg is placed in front of the outside leg. (*See* fig. 8, 29Ga.) The circle is the basis of the shoulder-in.

The rider:

a  Checks his position.

b  Increases the impulsion and collection, usually with a half-halt.

c  Increases the pressure of the inside leg just behind the girth.

d  Contains this extra impulsion by closing the fingers on the opposite (outside) rein and so preventing the horse from stepping straight forward.

e  Rests his outside leg a little further behind the girth than his inside leg to support the bend and stop the hindquarters swinging out; just as on a circle.

f  Keeps his shoulders parallel to the horse's, i.e., turns them to the inside.

g  Transfers slightly more weight onto the inside seat bone than the outside.

h  Keeps his inside seat bone forward.

When the shoulder-in is correctly ridden, it should be possible to abandon the inside rein for a few steps without the horse losing his balance, impulsion, or rhythm.

If and when the rider's outside hand allows the horse to move straight forward again, he should do so immediately and automatically return to a circle.

**15  Travers (quarters-in), and renvers (quarters-out)**: (Part Two, Chapter 4.54) In the travers and renvers the horse is slightly bent around the inside leg of the rider and positioned at an angle of about 30° to the line of the track. In travers the horse's hindquarters are towards the centre of the school or off the centre line (the forehand is on the centre line or outside track). In the renvers the horse's head is towards the centre of the school or the forehand is off the centre line while the hindquarters remain on the centre line or outside track. (*See* fig. 8.)

The rider:

a  Checks his position and adopts position left for left travers, and position right for right travers.

b  Applies his inside leg by the girth.

c  Applies stronger aids with his outside leg behind the girth to move the hindquarters slightly away out of line with the horse's forehand, but without reducing the forward movement.

d  Asks for the bend with the inside rein.

e  Controls the impulsion and any tendency for the shoulder to fall out with the inside rein.

f  Keeps a little more weight on the inside seat bone.

g  Keeps the inside seat bone forward.

The aids for renvers are identical, but the hindquarters are kept on the track and the forehand directed off it in the direction of the movement.

**16  The Half-Pass**: (Part Two, Chapter 4.55) This is a variation of travers which is executed on the diagonal. The horse is slightly and uniformly bent around the inside leg of the rider, and should be aligned as nearly as possible parallel to the long side of the school, but with the forehand slightly in advance of the hindquarters. The outside legs cross and pass in front of the inside legs. The horse looks in the direction in which he is moving, thus moving both forwards and sideways at the same time. (*See* fig. 8.)

The aids are similar to those for travers and renvers. The rider:

a   Checks his position and builds up the impulsion.

b   Asks for a bend with the inside rein.

c   Looks towards the point to which the movement is being made.

d   Applies the inside leg beside the girth to keep the horse moving forward and to act as a support around which the horse is slightly bent.

e   Applies with rhythmical variations in pressure the outside leg behind the girth to encourage both the horse's outside legs to step forward and across the track of the two inside legs.

f   Maintains a constant feel with the outside rein to control the impulsion and prevent the shoulders falling out.

g   Moves the inside seat bone well forward with the weight positively on it.

As the movement progresses the leg aids are gradually increased so that the horse is finally straight (i.e., parallel) to the track or wall before being ridden forward on one track, or before changing to a half-pass on the other rein. The half-pass can be ridden at all three paces.

**17  The Pirouette**: (Part Two, Chapter 4.56) This is a half circle performed on two tracks with a radius equal to the length of the horse. The forehand moves around the haunches. The forefeet and the outside hind foot move around the inside hind foot, which acts as the pivot, returning to the same spot or just in front of it each time it is lifted. (*See* fig. 8.)

The rider:

Applies the same aids as for the half-pass, but the outside leg may need to be a little stronger. The pirouette is the half-pass on the smallest circle.

Pirouettes and half-pirouettes may be ridden at the walk and later at the canter, but can only be done at the trot in piaffe.

## WORK AT THE CANTER

**18  Counter-canter or Contra-lead**: (*See* Part Two, Chapter 4.48.) The rider asks the horse to lead with the outside instead of the inside foreleg so that, e.g., when circling to the left the horse canters with the right lead.

The rider:
Uses the same aids as for the canter, maintaining the position towards the leading leg so that he will, for example, maintain position left when in counter-canter around a right turn. At first it may be necessary to hold this position more strongly, with the legs definitely applied and the weight positively on the inside seat bone, which is on the side of leading leg.

**19 Change of leg**: (Part Two, Chapter 4.49) To change the leading leg in the canter, the horse either does a simple change when he is brought back to the trot and/or walk and restarted into the canter with the other sequence of legs, or a flying change which is completed during the period of suspension in the canter when both fore and hind legs should change together, the leading leg initiating the change. **N.B.** In a dressage test a simple change is executed through the walk. The rider:
a   Checks his position.
b   Creates a little more impulsion, usually through the half-halt.
c   In the case of the simple change, after the walk or trot has been established, changes his aids from position left to right, or vice versa; similarly, for the flying change the aids are changed from position left to right, or vice versa, but just prior to the moment of suspension.
d   Ensures that his seat remains in the saddle as the aids are changed, but at the same time lightening and bringing forward into the new canter position the seat bone on the side of the leading leg.
TIMING: In the case of a simple change through another pace this is not difficult, but to perform a flying change this must take place during the moment of suspension which follows the use of the horse's leading foreleg. Only then are all four feet off the ground and only then can the horse answer the aids and change the leading hind leg and hence the sequence. Failure to give the canter change aid just before this moment often results in the horse only changing the leading foreleg and thus becoming dis-united. Once the rider has mastered this timing, repeated changes of leg may be carried out until the horse is changing every stride.

It is generally accepted that the rider's leg brushed back to behind the girth indicates which canter is required, but some well-known trainers prefer to emphasise the inside leg by the girth. In both cases, the timing must be correct.

## ADVANCED MOVEMENTS

**20   Piaffe**: (Part Two, Chapter 5.17) This is a highly cadenced, collected, elevated trot on the spot. The rider:

a Corrects his position.

b Uses both legs by the girth, either together or alternatively, to ride forward into a restraining but allowing light rein contact. The object is to ask the horse to bring both hind legs a little further under his body and so to lower his hindquarters and round his back.

c Sits lightly to allow the horse to round and move 'through' his back, but in an erect position with the seat bones forward to encourage forward impulsion.

d As the horse comes into piaffe, indicates the rhythm of the trot by increasing and decreasing the pressure of his legs, without removing them from the horse's sides. Once the horse has understood, the rider must be careful to take up the rhythm offered by the horse.

A well-trained horse in correct equilibrium will only require a light but consistent contact with the rein to hold it in piaffe, and should always be ready to move straight forward into passage or another pace.

At an intermediate standard, the horse should be allowed to gain ground in piaffe, but advanced horses should stay on one spot for 10–12 steps.

**21 The Passage**: (Part Two, Chapter 5.20) This is a very collected, elevated and cadenced trot. Each diagonal pair of feet is raised higher and with a longer period of suspension than for any other trot. The rider:

a Holds both legs firmly against the horse's sides and applies them in the rhythm of the pace. This should encourage the horse to move forward in a slow, supple and highly cadenced trot.

b Uses the reins to help control the pace and to a slight degree the balance.

c The rider sits deeply, but softly, in the saddle, in rhythm with the horse's pace so that both rebound together.

## PRACTICAL USE OF THE AIDS

**22** The aids and movements described in this chapter are in constant use in every form of riding, whether on the flat, jumping, racing, hunting, or when carrying out some more specialised activities, such as polo. The horse will often be required to carry out some of the schooling movements, not merely as an exercise, or part of a dressage test, but for strictly practical reasons. Thus, when hacking, besides the obvious necessity of the aids for changing direction or altering pace, the turn on the forehand, the pirouette and the rein-back, may be used, perhaps without conscious thought, when opening and closing gates. In the same way a rider may try to prevent the horse from shying by using the shoulder-in, so that the horse is bent away from the object he fears.

PART TWO

# Training the Horse

CHAPTER ONE

# The Paces

## INTRODUCTION

**1** To train a horse correctly it is vital to maintain and improve the purity of the paces rather than to create or fail to correct the numerous defects which develop in the horse's movements. Therefore, the trainer must understand the way the horse should move at the walk, trot, and canter, and for each of these paces the sequence of the leg movements is different as is the rhythm of the hoof beats.

## THE WALK

**2** **Rhythm**: Four hoof beats should be heard at equal intervals apart. The horse moves one leg after another so that the four hoof beats can be heard with the same period between each. Two or three feet are always on the ground at the same time, the horse stepping from one foot to another with no moment of suspension.

**3** **Sequence in which the legs leave the ground**: (*See* fig. 9.)
left hindleg; left foreleg; right hindleg; right foreleg.

**4** **The Aims**:
a    Rhythm of hoof beats is regular with the four hoof beats distinctly marked. A two-time walk (known as a pace or amble), or other losses of regular four-time hoof beats, are incorrect.
b    The strides are even and not hurried.
c    The strides are free, purposeful and unconstrained.
d    The head nods in the walk. The rider should not restrict this movement.
e    The legs are lifted, not dragged along the ground.
**N.B.** Faults in the walk are easily developed as there is little impulsion to help the rider maintain the rhythm of the pace. It is, therefore, not advisable to walk 'on the bit' during the early stages of training.

**9.** *The sequence of the footfalls at the walk.*

## THE TROT

**5    Rhythm**: Two hoof beats should be heard with the legs moving in alternate diagonal pairs, but separated by a moment of suspension. This moment of suspension is difficult for the rider to sit to and the problem can be avoided by rising out of the saddle as one of the diagonal pairs leaves the ground and returning to the saddle as this same pair comes back to the ground (rising or sitting trot).

**6    Sequence in which legs leave the ground**: (*See* fig. 10.)
a    Right foreleg and left hindleg
b    Left foreleg and right hindleg before the right foreleg and left hindleg touch the ground.

**7  The Aims:**
a   The rhythm of the hoof beats is regular (two-time).
b   The strides are even and not hurried.
c   The strides are light and have elasticity.
d   The hindquarters are engaged.
e   The joints flex and the limbs are not dragged.
f   The hind feet do not hit the fore feet (forgeing)
g   The head remains steady.
h   The hind legs are as active as the forelegs with the cannon bones of the forelegs and hind legs maintaining the same angle to the ground. The feet should always touch the ground towards which they are pointing so that there is no jerking of the limbs. (*See* fig. 11.)

**10.** *The sequence of the footfalls at the trot.*

**11.** *Exaggerated action of forelegs in the trot without the corresponding activity of the hindlegs.*

## CANTER

**8 Rhythm**: Three hoof beats should be heard and, like the trot, there is a moment of suspension when all four feet are off the ground.

**9 Sequence in which legs leave the ground**: (*See* fig. 12.)
When the right foreleg leads:
a   Left hindleg
b   Right hind and left foreleg together
c   Right foreleg followed by a moment of suspension.
When the left foreleg leads:
a   Right hindleg
b   Left hindleg and right foreleg together
c   Left foreleg followed by a moment of suspension.

**12.** *The sequence of the footfalls at the canter.*

When the canter is disunited (a fault) the forehand is on one lead and the hindquarters on another.

**10    The Aims**:

a    Rhythm of hoof beats is regular (three-time). Four hoof beats should not be heard, but often are when a horse is slowed down without sufficient impulsion.

b    Strides are even and not hurried.

c    Steps are light and cadenced.

d    Hindquarters are engaged with active hocks.

e    Balance is maintained.

f    Horse is straight with his shoulders directly in front and not to one side of his hindquarters.

g    It is a united canter (not disunited).

h    Head (and neck) do not nod up and down independently of the body (an indication of a lack of impulsion); but head moves in co-ordination with the horizontal action of the body. The horizontal movement occurs because when only the leading foreleg is on the ground the hindquarters must rise and the head tip towards the ground (*see* fig. 12), whereas at the end of the moment of suspension the hindquarters drop and the head rises. The result is a bounding action by the horse in the canter.

## GALLOP

**11    Rhythm**: This is similar to the canter but faster and with the diagonal sequence broken. It thus becomes a pace in which four hoof beats should be heard followed by a moment of suspension.

**12 Sequence in which legs leave the ground:**
When the left foreleg leads:
a Right hindleg
b Left hindleg
c Right foreleg
d Left foreleg followed by a moment of suspension.

**13 The Aims:**
a Rhythm of hoof beats is regular (four-time).
b Strides are even and not hurried.
c Balance is maintained although the centre of gravity is more forward.
d Horse is straight with his shoulders directly in front and not to one side of his hindquarters.

# VARIATIONS WITHIN A PACE

**14** A horse can be asked to extend and/or collect (that is, change the length of his strides and outline) at each pace. The extent of the variations within a pace depends upon the stage of the horse's training, and his own natural ability.

In the initial training, the horse has not the impulsion or suppleness to truly collect or extend, therefore at the trot and canter the working paces only should be asked for, and in the walk just the medium and free walk. As the training proceeds progressively more collection can be demanded and at the same time extension to achieve first of all the medium trot and canter and eventually, the extended walk, trot and canter.

**15 Aims within these variations:**
a The collection should result in shorter strides not slow ones, and for the extension longer strides not quick ones. Hurrying is one of the commonest faults when trying to extend the strides and leads to stiffening which can spoil the paces. It is nearly always caused by the rider asking the horse to extend before he has enough impulsion to be able to do so.
b The strides should be even, i.e., when the required length of stride has been achieved each stride should be maintained at this length, so that every stride is *even*.
c The rhythm of the hoof beats of a particular pace should remain true (the walk four-time, the trot two-time and the canter three-time), i.e., the pace should be *regular*.
d In all variations within a pace the horse should retain his willingness to go freely forward.

**13.** *The working paces, left at the canter, right at the trot.*

## WORKING PACES
(SEE FIG 13)

**16**   These are the paces which lie between the collected and medium. They are used particularly for horses not yet trained and ready for collected paces. Working walk is not recognised, but the working trot and canter are the paces from which respectively other trots and canters are developed.

AIMS AT ALL WORKING PACES:

a   To maintain the balance.

b   To keep the horse 'on the bit'.

c   For the hocks to be active, but this does not mean collection, only the production of impulsion from active hindquarters.

## MEDIUM PACES
(SEE FIG 14)

**17**   These are paces of moderate extension between working and extended.

AIMS AT ALL MEDIUM PACES:

a   Longer strides than for working, but rounder and shorter than for extended.

b   Unconstrained strides.

c   To produce lively impulsion from the hindquarters.

d   To keep the horse 'on the bit' (*see* Part Two, Chapter 4, 16 to 21) with the head and neck slightly lower than in the working and collected paces.

e    To extend the head more in front of the vertical than in the collected and working paces.

PARTICULAR FEATURES: At the medium walk the hind feet should touch the ground in front of the footprints of the forefeet (overtracking). This is the walk at which the rider first works the young horse.
At a good medium trot, as in the walk, the hind feet overtrack.

## EXTENDED PACES
### (SEE FIG 15)

**18**    In these the horse lengthens his strides to his utmost.
AIMS AT ALL EXTENDED PACES:
a    The strides to be as long as possible.
b    To produce lively impulsion from the hindquarters.
c    The horse to remain calm, and light in the forehand.

**15.** *The extended paces, left at the walk, centre at the trot, right at the canter.*

**14.** *The medium paces, left at the walk, centre at the trot and right at the canter.*

d   To keep the horse 'on the bit' with the head and neck lowered and lengthened so that the strides become longer, rather than higher.

e   Not to speed up so the strides become hurried.

PARTICULAR FEATURES: At the extended walk overtracking should be more pronounced than in the medium and the rider should allow the horse to stretch out his head and neck but without losing contact with the mouth. At the extended trot, as in the walk, the overtracking should be pronounced and there should be no flicking of the forelegs. (*See* fig. 11.)

## COLLECTED PACES
### (SEE FIG 16)

**19**   In these the strides are as short and high as possible and the horse is most manoeuvrable.

AIMS AT ALL COLLECTED PACES:

a   To produce lively impulsion from the hindquarters which are strongly

engaged with the joints well bent. This should result in a lightening of the forehand and the shoulders becoming more free and mobile.

b   To keep the horse 'on the bit' with his neck raised and arched so that there is an harmonious curve from the withers to the highest point – the poll. The head to be slightly in front of the vertical but may become more or less perpendicular when the rider uses his ·aids.

c   The hind legs to be engaged forward only insofar as they remain mobile. If placed too far forward, movement can be impeded.

PARTICULAR FEATURES: At the collected walk and trot the hind feet should touch the ground behind or in the footprints of the forefeet.


## FREE PACES

**20**   At these the horse is allowed complete freedom to lower and stretch his head and neck. He relaxes, but should remain active. The free walk is the most commonly used, especially for young horses, and as a reward for good work.

**16.** *The collected paces, above left at the trot, above right at the canter, right at the walk.*

CHAPTER TWO

# Lungeing

## INTRODUCTION

**1** Lungeing can be used throughout the training of the horse. As long as it is done well it improves the horse's physical co-ordination, developing his rhythm, balance, suppleness, willingness to go forward, and fitness; but probably even more important than this, it trains the horse's mind and can be a major influence on his mental outlook. Through lungeing the horse can be taught to respect, trust and obey his trainer.

**2** **Lungeing is used for**:
a   The initial training of the young horse.
b   Retraining spoilt horses.
c   Exercising horses which are not being ridden.
d   Settling and relaxing fresh or spirited horses before they are ridden.
e   Advanced dressage work.
f   To train the rider (*See* Part One, Chapter 2.).
   Lungeing is therefore a vital aspect of work with horses but demands a trainer with considerable experience, skill and ability to anticipate the horse's movements, if the horse is to derive full benefit from it.

## EQUIPMENT

**3**   **The Lungeing area**: (*See* Part One, Chapter 2.4.) An area of flat ground large enough for a circle of at least 20 metres (22 yds). It is an advantage if it is enclosed (sheep hurdles, poles, etc., can be used if an arena is not available), and is reasonably quiet so that the horse's attention can be maintained.

**4**   **The tack**:
a   A snaffle bridle, preferably with a simple snaffle bit which has quite a thick single-jointed smooth mouth piece. Either a drop or cavesson noseband is worn. If the reins are not removed they should never be attached to the stirrups or saddle, instead they can be twisted around

**17.** *The horse tacked up for lungeing. The figure shows how the reins can be twisted and held by the throat lash.*

under the neck and the throat strap put through one of the loops. (*See* fig. 17.)

b   *A Cavesson:* This has a padded noseband with three metal rings attached at the front and a cheek strap. The cavesson is fitted over the bridle and can be buckled either under the chin like a drop noseband, or above the bit like a cavesson noseband. The lunge rein is fastened to the central swivel ring on the noseband. The noseband and cheek strap should be tightened sufficiently to avoid the cheek strap being pulled round to rub the horse's outside eye.

c   A lunge rein of about 10 metres (33 ft) long, made of linen or nylon webbing with a large loop at one end and a swivel joint attached to a buckle or spring clip at the other.

d   Side-reins which should be about 2 metres (6 ft) long with a clip at one end and a buckle at the other. There should be a large number of holes at the buckle end so that there is scope for varying the length.

e   A roller with rings on either side to which the side reins can be attached.

f   A breast plate to stop the roller or saddle slipping back.

g   A saddle, possibly with numnah.

h   Boots that are worn on all four legs to prevent damage to them from knocks.

i   A lungeing whip with a thong which is long enough to reach the horse.


## LUNGEING TECHNIQUE

**5**   **The Trainer**: The trainer should wear gloves when lungeing so that if the rein is pulled quickly through his hands it will not burn. He should never wear spurs as these can trip him over.

The trainer who stands correctly will be more relaxed and able to react quickly to control the horse who suddenly pulls or turns. In the correct stance:

a   The upper body is erect.

b   The upper arms hang down with the hands relaxed and roughly at right angles to the body.

c   The legs are slightly apart and the knees relaxed.

**6   The Lunge Rein** should be held in the hand to which the horse is moving and the whip in the other. The end of the rein is looped (*see* fig. 18) so that it can be paid out without tangling, and the loops are held in whichever hand the trainer finds it easier to handle the rein efficiently and without getting it tangled.

**7   The position**: The trainer stands at an angle of about 45° to 50° to the horse's forehand with the horse's head just in front of his leading shoulder and himself in line with the horse's hips. He should concentrate on the movement in the horse's hindquarters rather than the forehand, aiming to drive the horse in a circle around him. Control over the hindquarters is vital if the trainer is to prevent the horse stopping or turning. The aim should be for the horse, the whip and the rein to form a triangle. (*See* fig. 19.)

The horse should describe a true circle so the trainer aims to stand on one spot, pivotting around one heel. With the young horses however, in order to remain in control it might be necessary for the trainer to shorten the rein, move closer to the horse and walk in a small circle.

Small circles are a strain for the horse, therefore a young horse should never be asked to describe a circle of less than 20 metres (22 yds) diameter. Only fit trained horses can be asked to lunge in a smaller circle.

**18.** *The first lesson in lungeing, when an assistant can be used.*

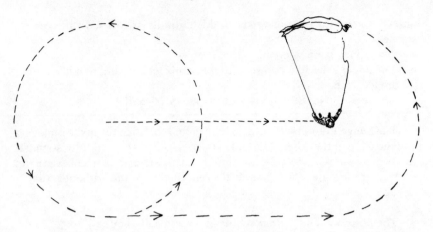

**19.** *Route of horse and trainer, when horse lengthens his strides or jumps on lunge.*

## THE AIDS

**8**   The aim is for these to simulate the aids used when riding. The lunge rein is equivalent to the reins; the whip to the legs, and the voice is used in conjunction with both these aids.

**9**   **The rein** should be used by the trainer to maintain a light, consistent contact with the horse and the aids applied with quick movements of the fingers or, if the horse starts to lean on the rein, by giving and restraining, but not pulling against him.

**10**   **The whip** is used as an aid and only in exceptional circumstances as a punishment. The horse should therefore be familiarised with it before lungeing and learn to accept it being rubbed along his side and hindquarters.
   During lungeing the whip can be applied if needed to make the horse move forward or increase the activity of the hindquarters. It should be flicked just above the hind fetlocks but quietly; the trainer should not lurch forward and loosen the rein. Normally the threat of the whip with a swing or a crack is sufficient.
   The whip is also used to keep the horse out on the circle. If he starts to cut corners or fall in, it can be pointed and, if necessary, flicked in the direction of his shoulder.

**11**   **The voice** is the aid used most frequently, minimising the use of the whip to make the horse go forward and use of the rein to make him slow

62

down. It is also used to soothe and calm the horse down and to help him establish a rhythm to his paces. The effectiveness of the voice is achieved by using it at first in conjunction with the rein and whip aids so that the horse learns that a sharp quick command 'walk on', 'trot', 'canter', means to move forward, and if low and drawn out 'whoaa', 'waalk', 'trrot', to reduce the pace. The tone of the voice is more important than the actual words used.

## THE WORK

**12**  It is advisable to start on the rein the horse finds the easiest (usually the left) although he should be worked equally on both reins.
*The time* spent on the lunge will depend largely on his stage of training, his fitness and the type of work on the lunge – he could walk for a long time but canter for considerably less. As a general rule five to ten minutes on each rein is sufficient for a green or unfit horse, and as he gets stronger and more balanced this can be gradually increased to a lesson of about ten to fifteen minutes on each rein. The horse must never be overworked otherwise he will lose his enthusiasm and/or might be physically strained.

## THE NOVICE HORSE

**13**  As soon as a horse is accustomed to wearing a bridle and cavesson, being led from both sides, and has learned to obey the voice aids to walk on and stand still, then he can be lunged.

For the first lesson it is advisable for him to wear the same tack in which he was led – just a snaffle bridle, cavesson and boots. The lunge rein is attached to the central ring on the cavesson.

**14**  **An Assistant**: It is advisable for all but the most experienced trainers to use an assistant during these first lessons. The assistant can then lead the horse from the inside of the circle with the lunge rein running through his hands to the trainer in the centre. (*See* fig. 18.) Once the horse has understood he is supposed to move around in a circle the assistant can move closer and closer to the trainer, and if the horse stays out, quietly walk out of the way. The same process should be repeated on the other rein.

**15**  **The Halt**: When the horse describes a true circle then he must be taught to halt and walk on when commanded. The horse should have learnt when being led that 'whoa' and vibrations on the rein mean to stop. These same aids should be applied on the lunge, taking care to control the hindquarters with the whip to prevent the horse from turning in towards the trainer. At first this may require the aid of an assistant.

The horse should halt on the outside of the circle (although some trainers do ask him to walk in towards them). He should not be asked to remain immobile for more than a few seconds. The trainer should then either ask him to walk on again or go out to him (keeping his whip behind him) to reward with pats, talking and occasional titbits.

If the horse does not halt remember it may not be through disobedience but misunderstanding, so be patient. If he persists then work him close to a high hedge or wall (that is unjumpable). If he does not listen to the command to halt/whoa, while keeping the horse between the whip and rein to stop him turning in or running down the wall, direct him towards the wall/high hedge, repeating the command. He will be forced to stop and when he does, make much of him.

**16    The Schedule**: There can be no time schedule for the lessons below. The horse should master each one in turn, and be able to remain calm, relaxed and obedient, before progressing to the next. The early lessons should be performed without side reins at a free walk and at a working trot. It is best not to canter until the horse is stronger, but if fresh he can be allowed to canter until he settles sufficiently to pay attention.

**17    The Stages**:
a    *To lunge with a roller:* The roller is fitted as in Part Two, Chapter 3.11, and the horse is lunged with it in place. The horse has to learn to relax and move freely with this restriction around his back and belly.
b    *Lungeing with a saddle:* When relaxed with a roller it can be replaced by a saddle. At first the stirrups should be removed. In a later lesson they can be run up, and finally prior to being backed allowed to hang free for a short time so that the horse gets used to being touched where the rider's legs will be.
c    *Lungeing with side reins:* These are attached a little above half way up the horse's side to either the roller or the saddle. (*See* fig. 20.)

To prevent them slipping down, the rings on the roller are preferable attachments. The side reins are made as long as possible and of equal length, then crossed over at the withers and attached to the D's on the saddle or roller. The horse is then lunged for a few minutes on both reins to supple up and relax.

The side reins are unclipped and most trainers then attach them directly onto the bit, but some advocate attaching them to the side rings on the cavesson for the first lessons. The horse is then lunged with the side reins so loose that he cannot feel their effect.

When he works calmly and rhythmically (it might be that lesson or two or three later), the side reins can be tightened, but making sure that they both remain of an equal length.

The side reins should be adjusted to the length that the horse makes contact with them when he engages his hindquarters, rounds his back and lowers his head. The aim is that as the horse has made the contact himself he will not fear it but will soon start to seek it and to chew gently at the bit.

The side reins should not be used to pull the horse's head into a particular position, nor should they be so tight that his head comes behind the vertical. (*See* fig. 20.) The horse's state of balance and way of going must always dictate their length. It is also dangerous for the horse to walk much with the side reins attached, as they restrict the natural movement of his head and make it more difficult to maintain the rhythm of the pace.

As the horse's balance improves he can bring his hind legs further underneath him, his outline becomes shorter and rounder and the side reins slacken. This is the time to shorten the side reins, but never so much that the horse stiffens and resists against them.

Some trainers only use of the side reins is for a brief period when familiarising the horse with the contact of the bit, prior to backing. They prefer to give the horse the freedom both to find his own balance and to stretch forward and down; this also avoids the danger of the horse resisting the contact by either hollowing his back and raising his head (above the bit) or getting over-bent and falling behind the contact (behind the bit).

**18 Straightness**: Young horses are not straight (*see* Chapter 4.14), but lunge work with side reins helps to reduce crookedness. This is not achieved by shortening the inside rein as this only swings the hindquarters to the outside which throws the weight onto the inside shoulder and tends to make

**20.** *Side reins correctly fitted on left; but too short on right.*

him want to bend to the outside and resist.

If the side reins are kept at the same length, when the horse places his inside hind leg well under him, which he must to turn in a circle, his weight will be transferred diagonally towards the outside shoulder. To maintain his balance he will turn his head and neck to the inside. The pressure on the outside rein becomes stronger and the mouth becomes moist on that side whereas the inside rein becomes looser.

**19  Variations of pace and paces**: The horse can be encouraged to extend the length of his trot stride, to do some medium trot (Chapter 1.17) and this is easiest for him if he is driven out of the circle onto a straight line and then returned into a circle in a different position when he can be brought back again into the working trot. (*See* fig. 19.)

The canter is introduced when the horse can trot with rhythm, has a willingness to go forward and moves with a supple swinging back. Its introduction should be a gradual process, the trainer asking at first for just a few strides on both reins. It is usually advisable to remove the side reins for the early lessons at the canter.

It is important that the trainer realises if faults are occurring at any of the paces (i.e., four-time canter). He should aim to improve the horse's paces all the time and to do this must have a clear picture of what is correct. (*See* Chapter 1.)

**20  Backing**: A horse which is relaxed when wearing a saddle and accepts the bit happily at the trot can be backed, but the more time spent on the lunge working, on the lessons below, the easier it will be for the rider to train the horse. It is however, advisable for the horse to learn to accept the weight of the rider before he gets too fit and strong. Many trainers therefore, back him while continuing with training on the lunge, i.e., lunge him for fifteen to twenty-five minutes before being ridden or alternating days of lungeing with days of riding.

## LUNGEING OVER OBSTACLES

**21  Lungeing over poles**: This helps to give variety to the work and encourages the young horse to lower his head, round his back and flex his joints.

The side reins are always removed for this work and for all jumping.

The horse is first led over the pole, and if he remains relaxed is then lunged at the walk and trot on a circle which is just short of the pole. When he relaxes he can be driven out of the circle and over the pole.

When lungeing over obstacles the trainer must ensure that:

a    The horse is presented straight at the pole and does not approach it at an acute angle which would encourage him to run out. This means that the trainer will have to move parallel to the pole and the horse will no longer describe a circle. (*See* fig. 19.)

b    The horse is given as much freedom as possible over the pole and is not restricted by the lunge rein from lowering his head.

c    The horse is driven from behind. The trainer should never get in front of him.

d    That the work is done in equal amounts on both reins.

e    The trainer allows the horse to take a number of straight strides upon landing and is not pulled straight back into a circle.

When the horse walks and trots in a relaxed manner over this single pole in both directions then the exercise can be extended. Poles can be scattered around the school over which he can be lunged, or poles can be laid in a series either in a straight line or round in a circle. They should be about 1.2 to 1.3 metres (4–4½ ft) apart. (*See* Chapter 6.15.) It is important that they remain at the correct distance and if a pole is displaced by the horse the poles should not be attempted again until correctly positioned. Heavy poles help to stop this occurring.

**22  Lungeing over raised poles**: When the horse trots over the poles in a relaxed manner, maintaining his rhythm and lowering his head, then raised poles on blocks can be introduced. The same techniques are used as for

**21.** *A well prepared obstacle for lungeing.*

poles on the ground (i.e., leading over, using single ones first and progressing to a series).

**23　Lungeing over a jump**: Ideally the wing stands of the fence should be low. A pole should be leant against the inside jump stand to prevent the lunge rein being fouled and to act as a wing. (*See* fig. 21.) With the poles on the ground the horse is led over the jump.

The horse is then lunged over the jump with the poles on the ground. When he does this calmly and without rushing, the end of the pole nearest to the trainer can be raised. When the horse is happy trotting over this another pole can be added to make a cross bar and after this a third bar laid along the top and later a fourth bar to make a parallel.

It is important to make this jumping fun for the horse so that the progress should be gradual, he should not be asked too much nor should the lessons be too long.

## ADVANCED WORK ON THE LUNGE

**24**　The main purposes of lungeing more advanced horses are:
a　As a means of loosening up horses which, in their preliminary work, stiffen against the weight of the rider.
b　As a visual aid to the trainer who can study from the ground whether his horse is going straight, has sufficient impulsion and suppleness, and that the paces are true.
c　As an aid to collection at the trot and canter. The horses can be gradually brought onto smaller and smaller circles (but never so small that he loses his rhythm or his back stops swinging), while the trainer asks for as much impulsion as possible. Then while maintaining this collection the horse is allowed to go back onto a larger circle.
d　As an aid to extension at the trot. The horse can be brought into a collected trot, as in c), then driven out of the circle onto a straight line, in the same manner as medium trot was asked for in paragraph 19 above.
e　Teaching piaffe (and very occasionally passage) in hand. This work is done on straight lines and is described in Chapter 5.18.

# CHAPTER THREE

# The Initial Training of the Horse

## INTRODUCTION

**1**   In the horse's natural state his instinctive defence is flight and he only fights if provoked. The aim of early training is to overcome his fear, to earn his trust and obedience, and turn the instinct of flight into a willingness to go forwards at all times.

Efforts to do this should start from the time a foal is born and, if well done in the early stages, will greatly simplify the horse's subsequent training.

## EARLY HANDLING

**2**   A foal should be properly handled from birth so that he learns to trust and respect humans and not to fear them. In the years before he is ridden he should be trained progressively to:

a   Lead quietly.
b   Be halter broken and tied up.
c   Be groomed and have the feet picked out and trimmed.
d   Accept the various items of tack used for breaking and riding.
e   Become familiar with and learn not to fear a variety of strange sights and sounds.
f   Obey the basic commands, i.e., 'walk on', 'whoa'.

## INITIAL TRAINING

**3**   When the horse is three or four years old he should have developed sufficiently, physically and mentally, to undergo the concentrated and progressive training of being backed, ridden and learning the aids.

THE STAGES OF TRAINING:
a   Leading in hand.
b   Lungeing.
c   Backing, i.e., teaching the horse to accept a rider on his back.
d   Being ridden on the lead and lunge.

e   Control by the rider.

*Feeding* during these stages must be carefully monitored. A young horse full of oats tends to be too spirited to understand and obey. It is vital to keep him sensible which usually means limiting his feed to nuts and bran (unless he is lazy and/or weak), and turning him out to grass whenever possible.

**5   The length of training** varies from horse to horse, depending largely on the horse's temperament, the extent and success of his initial handling and the ability of the trainer.

As a rough guide, and assuming his handling as a foal has been satisfactory, a professional trainer usually takes four to six weeks to lead, lunge, back and quietly ride a young horse. This refers to training at a school where cost, and therefore time, is usually an important factor.

It is essential that training should not be hurried. The horse should never be asked to carry out more than his condition or temperament warrant. Anyone wishing to train their own horse would be well advised to spend much longer on this early work. Extensive work on the lunge pays dividends later on, and six weeks is not too long.

## THE TACK
### (SEE CHAPTER 2.4.)

**6**   The following tack is needed:
a   A lungeing cavesson.
b   A snaffle bridle.
c   A linen or nylon webbing lunge rein.
d   A roller and breastplate.
e   A saddle, preferably with numnah and breast plate.
f   Side-reins.
g   Boots which should be worn on the forelegs in all work.
h   A neck strap, if a breast plate is not fitted.
A trainer needs a long lunge whip and should always wear gloves.

**7   Fitting the tack**: The items should be introduced one at a time, the horse being allowed to accept each new item quietly and with relaxation before another is tried.

**8   To fit a lunge cavesson**: This is buckled sufficiently tight to avoid it being pulled around. The lead/lunge rein is normally fitted to the central ring of the cavesson.

**9  To fit a bridle**: The snaffle bit must fit the horse's mouth so that it is neither so narrow that it pinches, nor so wide that the joint falls far down in the horse's mouth. The mouth piece should be quite thick and single jointed. Some horses object to having a bridle fitted, however carefully this is done, and in such cases the bridle may be put on like a head collar with the bit fastened to the off-side cheek piece only and allowed to hang down. The bit can then be put in the horse's mouth very gently before securing the near-side cheek piece tightly enough so that corners of the horse's mouth just wrinkle.

If the bit is too low the horse can easily get his tongue over it, if too high it will be uncomfortable.

**10  To fit the cavesson over the bridle**: (*See* Chapter 2, 4a and b.)

**11  To fit the roller**: Great care is necessary when first fitting a roller and later the saddle, as many horses are very disturbed by the restrictive feeling of the girth. One person is needed to hold the horse's head and to help with adjustments on the horse's off-side if a third person is not available. The trainer stands on the near-side and places the roller with the buckle end bent back over itself very gently on the horse's back. The breast plate is attached to prevent the roller from slipping back, before the buckle end of the girth is gently slid down the horse's off-side, quietly brought under the horse and drawn up to the retaining straps on the roller. It is attached very loosely at first, but if the horse is not upset it is gradually tightened by one or two holes at a time. It is advisable to move the horse forward a few steps between each tightening operation.

**12  To fit the saddle**: The same procedure is followed as for fitting the roller, including the attachment of the breast plate. Initially it is important that the girth is only just tight enough to prevent the saddle from slipping; if too tight the horse will often buck against the pressure.

## LEADING IN HAND

**13  The foal**: In most cases a horse is taught to lead in and out of his field or stable alongside his dam. To start with, the foal should be walked around his stable with a stable rubber around his neck, and a hand around his hindquarters. It is important to push rather than pull, helping to instil the willingness to go forward at an early age. Once he understands this, he may be led from a foal slip, but one hand should remain on or around the hindquarters, and it is this hand which deals with any arguments. The foal will soon learn that it is useless to resist and may then be led outside his stable, following his mother.

**14    The young horse**: If a young horse has missed this early training he can be taught to lead in a stable, preferably a large one, and it is best not to lead him outside until he is quiet and obedient on both reins.

A young horse should be led by a rein of about 3 metres (10 ft) fastened to the central ring of a lunge cavesson. When the horse is used to a bridle one may be worn under the cavesson, but the lead rein should never be attached to the snaffle bit as this may spoil his mouth.

**15    Assistance**: In the early stages, unless the horse has been taught to move freely forward as a foal, it is advantageous for the trainer to have an assistant walking behind the horse. He can then send the horse forward if he tries to stop or run back.

**16    Technique**: The trainer should walk beside, but not in front, of the horse's shoulder on the near-side and hold a whip in his left hand, which should be long enough to reach the hindquarters. If the horse draws back, or tries to stop, he can use his voice and the whip behind his back. (*See* fig. 22.) Often the threat of the whip is sufficient to make the horse obey, but if necessary it can be applied gently and, if not effective, more strongly.

**22.** *Use of the whip when horse is reluctant to be led forward.*

Forward movement, even too much, is of prime importance in the early and indeed, all stages of training. If the young horse, however, tries to hurry or run on too much, then repeated, rapid jerks on the front of the cavesson together with the voice, can be used to slow him down or stop.

When the horse is obedient to being led on the near-side he should be taught to go equally well from the off-side.

Before starting to lunge the horse should obey the commands to 'walk on' and 'whoa'.

## LUNGEING

**17**  Lungeing has a vital part to play in the training of the young horse, as long as it is done well. The last chapter described in detail the technique of lungeing.

## LONG REINING

**18**  In the past, long reining was widely practised as an alternative or supplement to lungeing, before backing was carried out. Although it enables a higher standard of training to be achieved, it requires special skills and needs an experienced trainer if the young horse is not to be spoilt. For this reason it is best left to the expert and it is not described in this book.

## BACKING

**19**  **The timing**: The trainer must decide when a horse is ready to be backed, according to each individual case. It is normally not attempted until the horse is obedient, relaxed and working well on the lunge.

If the preparatory work has been carried out correctly, the horse should accept the rider quietly and with confidence; conversely, a horse which reacts violently to being backed has almost certainly been inadequately prepared.

**20**  **The equipment**: Backing is best carried out in an enclosed place, such as an indoor riding school or a small paddock. The horse should be fitted with a snaffle bridle under the cavesson, a breast plate, and a saddle which most trainers prefer without stirrup leathers and irons.

**21**  **Assistance**: If possible, three people are used: the trainer, who usually holds the horse, an assistant, who helps the rider to mount and dismount and to maintain his position on the saddle, and the rider. With an experienced trainer, however, backing can and often must be done with two people and then the trainer both helps the rider to mount and holds the horse.

A useful aid is to place a straw bale beside the horse for the rider to use as a mounting block and to help accustom the horse to seeing a human above him.

**22  The stages**:

a   Before starting, the horse should be lunged to settle him down. When relaxed and calm, he should be led on the left rein alongside a wall or fence, but about a metre away, and halted. The trainer stands at the horse's head, on the near-side, holding him by the lunge rein which is attached to the cavesson. The rider, also on the near-side takes hold of the saddle, pats it, moves it gently about on the horse's back, jumps up and down a few times and then repeats this with one hand on the pommel and the other on the cantle. The whole procedure should then be repeated on the off-side.

b   If the horse remains calm, the trainer, or his assistant if he has one, can give the rider a leg up so that he can lean across the saddle. (*See* fig. 23.)

**23.** *Legging up the rider to lean across the saddle.*

This exercise is then repeated on the off-side. If the horse becomes upset, the trainer should comfort him and the rider can slide quietly to the ground. Whenever possible, the rider, whilst lying across the saddle, pats the horse on the opposite side. To reach this stage on the first day of backing is sufficient progress.

c   When the young horse accepts the rider leaning across the saddle from either side, he can be led forward a few steps, but this position is tiring for the rider and cannot be held for long.

d   The rider can then start to move around a little on the saddle, both at the halt and as the horse is led forward. He can also slowly raise his head and shoulders.

e   As the horse becomes confident the rider can put a leg over the saddle, taking care not to touch the horse's hindquarters to sit astride. The top part of the rider's body is still kept low, near to the horse's neck. This is done at the halt and when the horse remains calm he can be walked forward a few paces. The rider can then slowly raise his body so that the horse becomes used to him sitting upright.

At all times the rider and the trainer must be quick to reward the horse when he does well by patting him on the neck and praising him. Titbits should be avoided except as a reward at the end of the lesson.

## RIDING ON THE LEAD AND LUNGE

**23**   When first ridden the horse is led forward quietly, with the rider sitting upright but relaxed. Control is in the hands of the person leading who can pay out the rein and move away until the horse is on the lunge circle.

When the horse walks the circle calmly he can be asked to trot; at first when being led and then on the lunge. The rider starts in sitting trot with very little weight on the seat bones, but uses the rising trot as soon as his coming out of the saddle does not alarm the horse.

**24**   **Equipment**: Stirrups are used at the discretion of the rider; some prefer to use them from the start but with caution as they can get in the way and upset the horse by banging on his sides. The neck strap or breast plate is always worn and can be used by the rider to secure his position without interfering with the horse's mouth. The reins should be attached to the bit from the beginning, but only used in dire emergencies. Side reins should never be fitted.

**25**   **Introducing the aids**: If the horse remains calm when being led around the school or paddock with the rider on his back, the aids can be introduced. The trainer, holding the lunge rein loosely should encourage the horse to walk and halt, first in obedience to his voice and then to the rider's. The rider can then begin to introduce the rein and leg aids in conjunction with his voice. A schooling whip should be carried by the rider to reinforce when necessary, but with great care, the leg aids.

## CONTROL BY THE RIDER

**26** When the horse walks, trots, and halts calmly to the rider's aids the lunge rein can be removed. To ensure a smooth changeover after detaching the rein, the trainer continues to walk beside the horse, although leaving control to the rider, before moving away gradually.

The rider should concentrate on getting his horse to move forward calmly in answer to his aids, including the voice. When he wishes to make a turn he will have to rely on the use of the reins alone, moving a hand out boldly to the required side, but without any backward tension and still riding the horse forward.

Quiet, clear commands and firm but kind handling should produce results with the horse obeying the simple aids at walk and trot.

**27 Cantering**: There should be no hurry to teach the horse to canter with a rider. If started too early it can excite the young horse and may result in him losing his balance, even to the extent that the sequence of the pace and the length of stride is impaired.

To begin with, cantering should only be asked for on a straight line. On corners the horse should be allowed to fall back into the trot until repetition improves his balance and understanding of what is wanted. The rider merely takes up the correct position and gives encouragement until later when the more serious cantering lessons can start.

It is often easier for a young horse to canter if the rider adopts the basic position for jumping (Part One, Chapter 1.7), as this gives the horse's back more freedom.

**28 Standing still when mounted**: For safety and discipline it is essential that the horse should remain still when mounted, both when the rider is legged up and when he uses the stirrup.

An assistant trainer should hold the horse's head to ensure he does not move when the rider is legged up and first learns to accept the rider mounting with a foot in the stirrup. These first lessons are best done at the end of a session of riding so the horse is relaxed and even a little tired.

As soon as the horse is not disturbed by this manner of mounting, then the rider can mount using the stirrup at the beginning of a session, at first with an assistant holding the head, but after a few days without him. Then the rider must keep the horse immobile through use of the voice and, if necessary, the reins.

**29  Acceptance of strange objects**: An essential part of a young horse's training is to get him to accept strange sights and sounds without fear. Even as a foal coloured poles can be placed on the ground at the entrance to his paddock and he can be encouraged to follow his dam over them. It is beneficial too, to turn him out in a field from which traffic can be seen and heard.

TRAFFIC: Motor vehicles are a serious hazard today and great care must be taken to train the young horse to accept them calmly. It is important to take every possible precaution to prevent him from being frightened by lorries or cars. When riding outside for the first few times it is advisable to go with one or two trained quiet horses who can set an example and give confidence. At first the trained horse should be kept between the young horse and the traffic and if he remains calm, then the older horse can go in front of him, and eventually behind.

SHYING: If a horse shies at an object, he should not be beaten or forced too close to it, but allowed to pass by at what he considers a safe distance and with his head bent away from it. If each time he passes the object causing concern, the rider can quietly ask him to go a little nearer; the horse should overcome eventually his fear to pass it without shying. In this way any argument can be avoided and it is more likely that the cure will be permanent.

## SUMMARY

**30**  When a young horse is able to walk, trot, and canter calmly under the control of his rider, and has had regular ridden exercise for two to three months, then he should be sufficiently confident and physically fit to undertake the next stage of training which is considered in Chapter 4, 'The Basic Training of the Horse'.

# CHAPTER FOUR

# The Basic Training of the Horse

## INTRODUCTION

**1** A horse which has completed the training covered in Chapter 3, 'The Initial Training of the Horse', should be moving freely forward calmly and on a comparatively long rein in all three paces. The training covered in this chapter will help the horse to develop mentally and physically, increasing the scope of his natural ability so that he becomes a more pleasant ride and a better horse for competitions. It is training that can be used to improve the performance of every type of horse.

**2** **The basic training of the horse**:
a   Stimulates his willingness to go forward.
b   Develops his natural abilities.
c   Strengthens his physique.
d   Makes him more supple and gymnastic.
e   Increases his stamina.
f   Gives the rider more control.

## GENERAL PRINCIPLES

**3** The following are important:
a   *Avoidance of short cuts:* Training requires time, effort and patience. Short cuts, such as the use of gadgets, should be avoided as these develop resistances and create their own problems.
b   *Rate of progress:* Training cannot be conducted to a time-scale; it must be dependent on the progress made. This rate of progress will vary according to the ability and temperament of the horse and the rider. Although the trainer plans a programme for progressive training, it must be sufficiently flexible to suit the individual characteristics of the horse being trained.
c   *Use of reward and punishment:* The following system of training uses rewards and punishments, but no force, to teach the acceptance of the aids and obedience to the rider. The amounts of reward and punishment

will again vary according to the character of the horse. Hot-blooded, high-spirited horses usually need more rewards than lazy horses which might benefit from occasional reprimands; the trainer must analyse the character of his horse and apply the appropriate discipline. In all cases, however, persuasion is considered more effective than coercion. A frightened horse is too tense to learn. The aim must be willing co-operation obtained by rational ānd tactful methods, but at the same time there must never be any doubt as to who is in command; if authority and respect are lost, training stops.

## THE TRAINER/RIDER

**4** Since it is the rider who trains the horse it will be assumed throughout this chapter that the trainer is the rider.

*Qualities of a good trainer:*

a   Ability to make the horse understand. If the horse does not obey, the trainer must consider whether his instructions were understood. Before blaming the horse he should examine his aids and methods.

**N.B.** If a good basic position has been established by the trainer the aids can be given more clearly.

b   An understanding of the general nature of a horse and an ability to adapt his approach according to the temperament and individual characteristics of the horse he is training.

c   Patience and persistence.

d   The temper must always be controlled.

e   An air of calm authority when with the horse: ensuring all movements are quiet and deliberate.

f   Tolerance of playful high spirits in a young horse, but firmness in the face of wilful disobedience.

g   A good sense of rhythm.

h   A sufficient knowledge of horsemastership to know whether his horse is being well cared for and suitably fed.

## EQUIPMENT

**5**   This should include:

a   A snaffle bridle on which a drop or cavesson noseband can be used.

b   A long schooling whip which can be used to reinforce leg aids.

c   Brushing boots to be worn on the forelegs.

d   An enclosed area, preferably on good going for the flat work.

## OBJECTIVES OF TRAINING

**6** The following objectives are the basis of all training. It is difficult to place them in order of priority because they are inter-related with improvements to one being dependent upon, and having repercussions on, other objectives. Also, as methods of achieving them overlap, several may be worked on simultaneously and as each horse has different strengths and weaknesses the importance of work on a particular objective will vary. The seven objectives are:

a   Controlled forward impulsion.
b   Rhythm (and balance).
c   Suppleness.
d   Straightness.
e   Acceptance of the bit.
f   Submission.
g   Development of the paces.

## CONTROLLED FORWARD IMPULSION

**7** 'Impulsion is a tendency to move forward with elasticity, originating from the haunches, flowing into a swinging back and ending in the mouth' (Colonel Handler). It is contained energy created by the activity of the hindquarters and should be instantly ready for the rider to call on. The consequent willingness and ability of the horse to go forward is the foundation for all work. If impulsion is lost then it should be recreated before other movements are attempted.

**N.B.** Impulsion is not speed. A horse which has impulsion should be able to establish a slower rhythm to his paces and most impulsion is needed for trotting on the spot as in piaffe.

**8** **To develop impulsion**: The first step is to develop the basis of impulsion – the willingness to go forward. Until the horse goes forward to the aids it will be difficult to control him (a stationary horse cannot be steered and a lazy/slow one only with difficulty). The horse must therefore, be made responsive to the leg – to be in front of the leg – and leg aids can if necessary, be supported by the voice and taps with the whip. As the training progresses and the horse gains his rhythm and balance, more forward momentum can be created and the seat aids can be brought into action. This forward momentum, instead of producing more speed, can be partly contained within the horse (impulsion), as the driving aids instead of simply making him go forward can, if the rider's hands restrain but allow, result in the horse's hindquarters becoming more engaged and active. This gives the horse the power to go forward as soon as he is asked.

In creating this forward impulsion it is important that it is not associated with speed. He should never be asked to go forward so much that he begins to lose balance and goes faster, nor should so much impulsion be created that the rider cannot control it, for then the tendency is to pull the reins backwards, which destroys the impulsion and creates resistance.

## RHYTHM (AND BALANCE)

**9** Rhythm is the regular recurrence of a given time interval between one footfall and the next in any of the paces. Each pace has its own rhythm. The walk is four-time (1–2–3–4), the trot is two-time (1–2, 1–2), and the canter three-time (1–2–3).
**N.B.** Tempo should be distinguished from rhythm. It is the speed of the rhythm: the time it takes for a sequence of the footfalls to occur. Cadence is when a pace has pronounced rhythm. (*See* paragraph 24 below.)

**10 Importance of rhythm**: As in so many spheres of life (athletics, art, etc.) rhythm is vital to make best use of ability. When a horse has rhythm he will also be balanced and so find it easier to remain calm and relaxed. Many trainers find rhythm the clearest and easiest primary objective. When it is achieved the horse should be balanced, calm and relaxed.

**11 To develop rhythm**: The aim is to get a horse to maintain the rhythm of a particular pace on straight lines and through corners. To do this he must be balanced.

A horse has natural balance when moving freely in his paddock, but when he starts to be ridden the weight of the rider puts him on his forehand, if he maintains his natural balance this will make it difficult to keep a rhythm. The hindlegs will tend to push the weight rather than lift it, which will usually make the paces flat, heavy and irregular. To be balanced, in a rhythm when carrying a rider, the horse has to engage his hindlegs bringing them further underneath his and the rider's body. To achieve this, the rider applies short but repeated driving aids with legs, and later the seat, asking the horse to go forward to a restraining but allowing hand, and at the same time the rider must think of the rhythm of the pace.

## SUPPLENESS

**12** A horse must be supple in order to be a comfortable ride and to make best use of his physique. The aim is a suppleness which allows the relaxed co-ordination of every muscle and joint. Tension is the major restriction on such an aim for whether it is caused by excitement, apprehension, or resistance, it not only reduces concentration but inhibits the freedom of movement. To be supple the horse should be calm and relaxed. The most common area of tension is the back for the horse naturally tends to stiffen and become rigid under the weight of the rider. This makes it difficult for the rider to sit in the saddle, to apply his seat aids and to feel the actions of the horse, and for the aids to come 'through'. (*See* paragraph 22 below.)

The horse's back should be supple and 'swing' so that the muscles behind the saddle move in unison with the horse's legs to provide an elastic connection between, and so co-ordinate the hindquarters and the forehand. At the walk, sitting trot and canter, the trainer must be supple enough to enable the horizontal and vertical movement in the horse's back to occur. (*See* Part One, Chapter 1.6.)

**13  To develop suppleness**: Whilst maintaining the rhythm (rhythm reduces inhibiting tensions) the horse is made more supple by gradual stretching. He must learn to bend slightly around the rider's inside leg on curves so that his body is bent to the curvature of the line he is following. This is achieved through work on circles, serpentines and loops, and later, in lateral work.

Those vital back muscles can be made more supple, especially in the early stages, by longitudinal stretching – 'to show the way down', so that the back is stretched and comes up (convex cf., hollow outline), as when basculing over an obstacle. (*See* fig. 24.) This is best done on a circle using

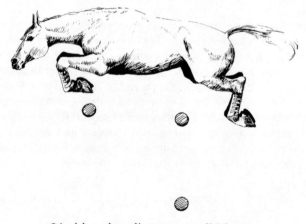

**24.** *A horse basculing over a parallel fence.*

soft half-halts to the left and right, then giving (not restraining) with the reins. The horse should soon start to 'seek the bit', reaching down and going forward to the hand with the rider encouraging even great engagement of the hindquarters. It is vital that the rhythm is maintained and the hindquarters are engaged so that the horse is not 'shown the way down' at the expense of falling onto his forehand.

**N.B.** Some schools do not support 'showing the way down' because of the danger of the horse falling onto his forehand.

Other important suppling exercises are frequent, well-executed transitions, encouragement of the willingness to go forward, use of trotting poles and small fences and, later, lateral work.


## STRAIGHTNESS

**14** The horse is straight when the hindlegs follow the tracks of the forelegs, which means he will be straight when moving on straight lines and slightly bent from nose to tail along the line of the curve on curved lines. There should not be any greater bend in the neck than the rest of the body.

**15 To make the horse straight**: The untrained horse is rarely straight and the rider will feel that the horse accepts the rein contact more readily on one side than on the other. The hindleg will be more bent on the hollow side and will not truly follow the track of the corresponding foreleg. Therefore, the shorter muscles on the hollow side have to be stretched, but gradually, to avoid strain and stress. Forcible bending of the neck produces tension, resistance and tilting of the head. It is important not to concentrate entirely on the forehand as the hindleg which is slightly left behind must be encouraged to come forward and under the body.

It is difficult to make a horse truly straight until he is capable of performing the best of all straightening exercises – the shoulder-in. By this stage too, the hindquarters will be more engaged and the shoulders easier to control. Therefore, not too much emphasis should be placed on straightening the young horse, but the following is excellent preliminary work. If the horse is stiff to the right and hollow to the left he will be slightly bent in his whole body around the rider's left leg and may tend to bend his neck too much to that side. With such a horse the trainer begins his schooling sessions riding on the left rein which is the easiest for the horse and concentrates at first in preventing him from bending his neck too much to the left. Contact with the left rein is maintained while using short, gentle taking and giving actions with the right rein to reduce the excess bend in the neck. At the same time the trainer uses his leg (and seat) aids to push the horse forward into the hand to obtain an even and momentarily stronger contact (a very green horse will rarely take enough contact to do this). It is important (as in all work) that the use of the seat and leg aids and the maintenance of the will to go forward are kept uppermost in the mind during these straightening exercises. An excess of rein aids leads to resistances and the horse dropping behind the aids.

After several circuits the rider should change the bend and repeat the same lesson on the more difficult rein for the horse. Equal amounts of work should be done on both reins.

**N.B.** The rider should gradually experience a more even feel on the reins and have less difficulty in correcting the bend in the neck, but it is a slow process as muscles must develop to enable the horse to get straighter. The aids for correcting a stiffness to the right would be reversed if the horse is stiff to the left.

The problem of one-sided stiffness has to be dealt with throughout most horse's training. At times the feel on both reins may be equal then the following day slight stiffness on one side may be felt.

## ACCEPTANCE OF THE BIT

**16** The horse accepts the bit when he maintains a light elastic rein contact with the rider without resistance and with submissiveness throughout his body. When jumping, riding out, or in early stages of training, he may accept the bit without fulfilling the conditions necessary to be 'on the bit'.

**17  A horse is on the bit if:**
a   The hocks are correctly placed.
b   The neck is more or less raised and arched according to the stage of training and the extension or collection of the pace.
c   He accepts the bit without resistance, with a light and soft contact, a relaxed jaw and submissiveness throughout his body.
d   The head remains steady and, as a rule, slightly in front of the vertical.
e   A supple poll is the highest point of the neck.

The rein contact should not be hard and solid, nor should it be so light that it is like holding a thread. A correct contact means a consistent elastic easy tension that comes from a forward tendency originating in the hindquarters and passes 'through' a relaxed and swinging back, the neck and so to the mouth, where it is accepted evenly on both sides. Such a contact is only possible when the horse is in balance, carrying himself and not relying on support from the reins. Balance and contact are therefore complimentary – the better the balance, the better the contact, and vice versa.

**18** **To accept the bit**, the horse should be:
a  Worked so that he develops a constant willingness and ability to go forward (impulsion).
b  Trained so that he is straight and accepts the same contact on either side of his mouth.
c  Encouraged to 'seek the bit' from really quite an early stage of his education.

The trainer should, as soon as possible, take a light but positive and continuous contact with the bit through the reins. By keeping the horse calm and in rhythm, using an 'asking' leg, and 'allowing' hand, but without losing contact, the rider should soon induce the horse to move forward onto the bit. The horse can be allowed to carry his head in a natural position as long as the rider follows the mouth to maintain a light contact with a forward, not pulling tension, through the reins. The rider should, in effect say, 'this is my hand and you must accept it', so the horse finds that the hand is acceptable and there is no point in resisting it.

The trainer should never use the reins to place the horse's head in a particular position. The horse uses his head and neck to balance himself. A horse will place his head in accord with his conformation, the stage of training he has reached, the flexibility of all his joints and the activity on his hindquarters.

**19** **If the horse pulls** on the reins in an effort to go faster, then the trainer should, with many downward transitions and repeated giving and taking actions of the reins, make him accept a balance and rhythm on a lighter contact.

**20** **If the horse is above the bit** (*See* fig. 25) then his head is held high, the angle of the head is too far in front of the vertical and his back will tend to hollow. Such a horse should be given the exercises (paragraph 13 above) to develop a stronger and more rounded back. He is usually best worked at the rising trot, or in bad cases, at the walk. The rein contact should be particularly sympathetic, the rider trying to feel with his hand, to get the horse to bend his poll, relax his lower jaw and stop resisting the contact. The horse should be ridden forward to a rein contact and asked to engage his hindquarters which will encourage him to round his back and lower his head. This is especially effective when working on a circle when the trainer can ride positively to the outside rein asking intermittently with an open inside rein for the bend and allowing as soon as there is any submission to the outside rein (Part One, Chapter 3.9). The reins should not be used to pull the head down as this forces the hindquarters backwards and create resistances.

**25.** *A horse going above the bit.*

**21  If the horse is behind the bit** (*See* fig. 26), he holds his head low and behind the vertical. This can be due to the rider's hands being too strong, his legs and seat too weak to drive the horse up to the hand, or the horse being asked to collect without enough impulsion. It is corrected by riding the horse forward to a positive contact and with a forward tension on the reins. This contact is lightened when the horse accepts the bit correctly.

Many horses will during training, drop behind the vertical. This is not a serious fault as long as he is not trying to avoid the contact but is maintaining a light, elastic consistent feel with the hand. This tendency does however, become serious if it is allowed to persist for a long period.

## SUBMISSION

**22**  The rider gradually increases his control over the horse to make him mentally willing and physically capable of obedience. The aim is a horse 'on

**26.** *A horse dropping behind the bit.*

the aids': when he accepts the aids in a relaxed manner and submits without resistance to the will of the rider. This submission does not mean a reluctant subservience, but the establishment of a harmony between horse and rider.

The horse should learn to accept the aids from the legs without tension, the seat of the rider without stiffening, and from the reins without resistance. For these aids to be effective and their co-ordination possible they must go 'through' the horse, i.e., the horse's hindquarters, back, neck and mouth are co-ordinated and connected by an elastic-like circuit so that the aids applied in any of the areas will be felt in all the others. If this firm elastic connection is blocked at any point by stiffness, tension, or resistance (i.e., is not submissive throughout the body), then the aids will not go 'through' and cannot be harmoniously combined. Also the horse's movement will be short of his best and any collection will tend to be a slowing down rather than a shortening and heightening of the steps.

**23   To develop submission**: To achieve mental submission the rider has to

EQUITATION

establish a rapport with his horse, and be able to communicate with him. To do this he must:

a  Understand his horse – analyse his character, become aware of his physical strengths and weaknesses.

b  Give the horse the best opportunity to understand, i.e. be able to ask clearly, to apply the aids effectively, and Part One, Chapters 3 and 4 should be thoroughly studied to achieve this end.

To achieve physical submission the horse must develop impulsion, rhythm (and balance), suppleness, straightness and accept the bit, so that he will find it easy to work 'with' and not 'for' his rider.

## IMPROVEMENT OF THE PACES

**24**  The paces should improve as the above objectives are developed. It is important, however, that the rider has a clear idea of what is correct (Chapter 1); then he can stop faults occurring, correct any that have, and aim to improve the natural paces. At the trot and canter one of the aims must be to make these paces more cadenced, i.e., to develop a pronounced rhythm, rhythm with energy to give more bounce to the strides through greater flexion of the joints and engagement of the hindquarters.

## SUMMARY

**25**  The above objectives should be borne in mind throughout the basic training of the horse. They should be the end products of the work which has been divided into two stages – preparatory and intermediate.

## PREPARATORY STAGE

**26**  This stage of training (lasting four to twelve months, depending on the ability of the horse and trainer) aims to produce a horse which:

a  has fine, regular and unhurried paces;

b  is calm, relaxed and obedient to the aids of his rider;

c  shows a good natural outline, balance and rhythm;

d  moves freely forward, without collection, but with active hindquarters;

e  accepts the bit willingly, without tension or resistance;

f  remains straight when moving on straight lines and bent accordingly when moving on curved lines;

g  executes transitions smoothly and remains still when halted;

h  is a pleasure to ride in the school and out of doors.

## THE WORK

**27** This should include:
a  Work on the flat.
b  Gymnastic jumping exercises.
c  Riding out, including hill work.

## WORK ON THE FLAT

**28** **Pattern of work**: It is best to start at the rising trot on the horse's easiest rein and then to change the direction frequently (remembering to change diagonals, Part One, Chapter 2.16). The first part of the work is aimed at loosening up and relaxing the horse.

All the work should be done on both reins and approximately equal time should be spent on each rein.

Frequent rest periods at the walk on a long rein are needed and it is wise to finish on a good note performing a movement that the horse can do well.

When the horse trots with lively steps and a relaxed swinging back he should begin to present a degree of roundness in his outline, with the poll at the highest point of his neck. When he has reached this stage he is ready for the sitting trot and to canter.

**29** **Duration**: Half an hour to fifty minutes, or two sessions of thirty minutes are average sessions, but it depends greatly on the strength and temperament of the individual horse.

## THE FIGURES

**30** From this early stage of training it is important to get into the discipline of executing accurate figures. The circles should be round, the straight lines straight and the horse taken as deep into the corners as is possible without him losing impulsion, rhythm, correct bend and the willingness to go forward.

The circles should be limited to 20 metres (22 yds) in diameter, the half-circles of 15 metres (50 ft) in diameter and the loops of a serpentine to a 12 metre (40 ft) diameter.

## THE PACES

**31** These should be limited to a free walk on a long rein, the medium walk, a working trot and working canter. (*See* Part Two, Chapter 1.)

**32** When the horse is ready to canter (*see* paragraph 28 above) he must learn to strike off on the correct leg. The easiest position to do this is either when on a circle, or on a figure of eight as the bend is changed into a new direction. If he strikes off on the wrong leg he should not be brought back to a halt, which he might regard as a form of punishment, but just to a trot and the strike off tried again. If, for any reason, the horse when asked to canter, goes into a fast trot, he should not be allowed to strike off until brought back into a calm, relaxed working trot.

Cantering is difficult for a young horse, especially on the circle and should not be continued for too long. Many young horses find it easier to canter with their backs rounded and relaxed if the trainer is in a jumping position with his seat bones just out of the saddle.

## THE TRANSITIONS

**33** These should be progressive, i.e., from canter to walk not directly, but through trot, similarly with upward transitions. In these early stages of training, the manner in which a transition is executed is more important than its achievement at a given marker.

Transitions should be carried out smoothly, but not abruptly. If the horse does not respond, ask again and again if necessary, so that the aids are repetitive, not continuous. For a transition to be satisfactory, the horse must be balanced as he goes into it and have sufficient impulsion. The rhythm of pace should be maintained up to the moment the pace is changed, or the horse is halted, and established in the new pace as soon as possible.

a *Upward transitions* (Part One, Chapter 4.3a) It is vital that the rider prepares the young horse for an upward transition and, in particular, developing enough impulsion to enable the horse to obey without throwing his head in the air, or hollowing his back.

b *Downward transitions* (Chapter 4.5) These must be ridden into, the trainer maintaining his correct seat and using a restraining but allowing hand. If he pulls backwards on the reins he will create resistances and stiffen the horse's back. In the early stages it is helpful to use the voice to avoid having to pull on the reins.

## MOVEMENTS

**34** These should be limited to the halt, the turn on the forehand and an elementary understanding of the half-halt.

## THE HALT
### (PART ONE, CHAPTER 4.6)

**35** It is important from the beginning of the ridden work, that the novice horse should be taught to stand still when halted. Initially he should be halted largely through use of the voice and with a light contact on the bit; for a second or two he should not move his head or legs. The novice horse should not be asked to stand still for too long; about three seconds is enough.

Too much importance should not be attached to the novice horse standing square. One hindleg is often left behind a little and it is better that the rider himself remains still, rather than tries to correct the fault which usually disappears as the horse becomes more supple. Not until the horse readily accepts the bit and is really going forward, will he be able to bring his hindlegs sufficiently under him to establish his balance and stand with his weight equally adjusted over all four legs.

## THE HALF-HALT
### (PART ONE, CHAPTER 4.7)

**36** This is a hardly visible moderated version of the halt, which:
a   Increases the attention and balance of the horse.
b   Helps to engage the hindquarters, generate impulsion, and lighten the forehand.
c   Warns the horse that the rider is about to ask something of him.

To be effective, the rider must, as in all the work, get the horse to think forward, i.e., the driving aids are more important than restraining aids. The seat and leg aids are applied to produce more activity in the hindquarters which should have repercussions on other muscles in the horse's body (i.e., the muscles are co-ordinated, so the aids go 'through' and are not isolated to the hindquarters). To stop, the driving aids simply increase the horse's speed, but the reins momentarily restrain. This results in the increased energy and attention produced by the driving aids being contained with the horse, to result in a, b, and c above.

If the half-halt is to be effective, the back must be relaxed and swinging to enable the aids to go 'through' and allow the back to perform its function of acting as a connecting link between the forehand and the hindquarters. If the back is stiff, tense, etc., then the rein aids cannot go 'through' and the tendency will be for the horse to raise his head, hollow his back and lose the compressing effect of the half-halt.

After applying the rein aids the rider then gives momentarily with the hands so that the horse learns to hold himself together and does not rely for support on the reins. The rider should aim to (in the Intermediate stage), hold his horse with his seat and leg aids without reliance on the reins.

The half-halt becomes more important as training progresses, but the young horse should be gradually introduced to its aids and learn to accept them correctly.

**N.B.** Not all schools use the half-halt.

## TURN ON THE FOREHAND
### (PART ONE, CHAPTER 4.13)

**37** In this movement the horse's hindquarters rotate around the forehand, the bend either away from the direction of the movement, or alternatively, in the direction of the movement. (*See* figs. 8 and 29g.) It is the easiest movement to teach the horse obedience to the lateral aids and can, therefore, be introduced at an early stage. It also helps to make the back supple.

AIMS:

a   Purposeful movement of the hindlegs around the forelegs.
b   To neither step backwards, nor forwards.
c   Forelegs to move in a very small circle.

EXECUTION: From a halt to move right, apply left leg behind the girth and feel on the left rein to bend the horse slightly in that direction.

## GYMNASTIC JUMPING EXERCISES

**38** These are discussed in detail in Chapter 6.

As soon as the horse has learned to accept the bit, and to walk, trot, and canter without excitement, he should receive elementary jumping lessons. They are valuable in teaching the horse to use himself athletically, thereby strengthening his muscles and making him both supple and mentally alert.

They can be given about twice a week and, if possible, on good going. At this novice stage the jumps should be used to give a horse confidence and should never be too large. Working up from little fences to about 1 metre (3 ft 6 in.) in height, with a maximum of a 1.5 metres (5 ft) spread. Grids with accurately measured distances between the obstacles are initially the most valuable.

## RIDING OUT

**39** It is vital to keep a young horse's interest. He will soon tire of school work if he is weak and finds it an effort. Riding out, especially hill work, will help to develop his muscles as well as providing him with the variety which will be mentally refreshing.

Frequent riding out is, therefore, advisable, but the objects of training can still be kept in mind. Hacking across fields, over undulating ground, along lanes, need not be time off, but another opportunity to develop the objectives of basic training.

In this outside work control is vital. It frightens the horse and rider if this is lost, so that a trainer must gauge how much can be asked of his pupil. He should not ask a nervous horse to go through heavy traffic or a busy town without the company of another more reliable horse. If going for a canter he should sense when the horse is showing signs of 'coming to the boil', and ease the pace before he loses control; then the occasional gallop can be enjoyed with safety.

Visits to horse shows where a young horse can get used to crowds, other horses and strange sights, are a useful experience.

Towards the end of this stage of training, a day or two out with the local hunt can be beneficial, especially for potential eventers or jumpers who need to get accustomed to different obstacles, and for lazy horses to develop impulsion.

After riding out, the trainer should examine his horse in the stable for possible damage and to assess his general condition.


## THE INTERMEDIATE STAGE

**40** The intermediate stage is a continuation of the preparatory stage, further developing the objectives of training but with increasing emphasis being placed on collection.


## COLLECTION

**41** Collection (Chapter 1.19) becomes an important objective at this stage, but it is only possible to develop if the trainer maintains and improves the other objectives of impulsion, rhythm, suppleness, straightness, acceptance of the bit, submission and good paces.

BENEFITS OF COLLECTION

a   The development and improvement of the balance of the horse.
b   The engagement and lowering of his hindquarters, which will lighten and make his forehand more mobile. This enables the strides to become longer or higher, as desired.

c   The horse will develop more ease and carriage in his work which will make him more pleasurable to ride.

Thus, the horse should become more manoeuvrable, more able to generate the power to extend his paces, carry out dressage movements, or jump fences.

TO COLLECT: Collection is achieved by greater engagement of the hindquarters, and not a slowing down to produce trudging, inactive steps. Impulsion must be maintained, or even increased, when asking the horse to shorten and heighten his strides into collection.

The major aids for collection are half-halts, increasingly small circles, serpentines, variations within a pace, smooth direct downward and upward transitions and lateral movements.

## THE WORK

**42**   This should include:
a   Work on the flat
b   Gymnastic jumping exercises
c   Riding out, including hill work and some strong canters on good going
d   Competitions. If possible, occasional participation in such competitions as a One-Day Event of the type organised by the Riding Clubs, or Novice and Elementary Dressage tests, or Novice Showjumping. These would give independent assessments of the progress being made.

## WORK ON THE FLAT

**43**   The work entails first loosening up and stretching the muscles, then flexing them into collection. When asking the horse for an effort the trainer must first be certain of the aims and if the horse is physically and mentally ready for the co-operation needed. If problems arise then revert to the basic principle of 'straighten your horse and ride him forward', as so many difficulties arise from loss of impulsion and crookedness.

The work must continue to be progressive, using the figures and movements below to improve the objectives of training. Thus from merely learning to remain immobile the horse can be taught to halt square, and rein back; from the easiest lateral work of the turn on the forehand and leg yielding progress to the shoulder-in and half-pass; and from canter work at the counter-canter and use of simple changes progress to flying changes.

Nor should just the movements tackled be progressive but also the manner in which they are performed. Thus, the trainer progresses from achieving just a few steps of a movement to quite lengthy pieces of the movement; from performing such things as shoulder-in with little collection and angle to achieving the desired 30°; from trying half-pass with very little bend to asking for a good deal of bend and sideways movement. Although trainers can keep in mind how Grand Prix horses perform movements they must realise that it takes considerable muscular power and suppleness to do them this way. These can only be developed with progressive work. Also, few eventers or show jumpers would be able, or willing, to develop the collection needed for the best manner of performance.

## THE FIGURES

**44**  The trainer can gradually reduce the sizes of the circles as more collection is achieved to 10 metres (33 ft) diameter, and half-circles of 6 metres (20 ft) diameter. The circles for the medium trot and medium canter should not be smaller than 20 metres (22 yds) diameter, and the extended canter should be ridden along straight tracks.

Serpentines are an excellent suppling exercise, especially if pear-shaped (as in fig. 27). The size of the loops can be gradually reduced. The serpentine can be used in trot, and canter with simple changes on the centre line, or some counter-canter loops.

(For other useful figures *see* figs. 28 and 29.)

## THE TRANSITIONS

**45**  Frequent transitions from one pace to another, and transitions within the pace help to achieve the objectives of training, as long as they are performed correctly.

When working on one track the trainer can gradually increase the degree of collection in his horse and alternate this with successively the medium and extended paces.

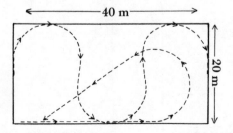

**27.** *Diagram of a serpentine and a 15 metre half circle; exercises which are useful for the novice horse.*

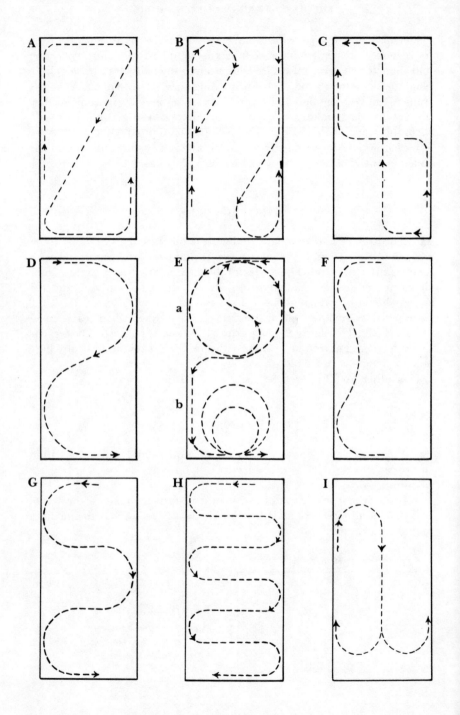

Transitions of two levels up, e.g., halt to trot, walk to canter, can be executed together with similar downward transitions.

The transitions should be made more quickly and less progressively than in the preliminary stage.

THE AIMS:

a   To show a clear transition;

b   To be quick, but smooth and not abrupt;

c   To maintain the rhythm of the pace up to the moment the pace is changed, or the horse halts;

d   For the new pace to be true and to show lively impulsion. This is only possible in downward transitions if made by riding forward into a restraining but allowing hand. The horse should gradually learn to accept the aids from the seat and legs rather than the hands;

e   For the horse to remain 'on the bit', light in hand, and calm.

## THE HALT
### (PART ONE, CHAPTER 4.6.)

**46   The Aims**: At the halt in the preliminary stage the horse was first and foremost immobile, but not necessarily four square. Now the aims should be:

a   To distribute the weight evenly on all four legs which are pairs abreast of each other (a square halt);

b   To hold the neck so that the poll is the highest point and the head is slightly in front of the vertical;

c   To remain 'on the bit' and maintain a supple jaw;

d   To remain motionless, but attentive, and ready to move off at the wish of the rider.

TO EXECUTE: The horse's weight has to be transferred to his hindquarters by increasing the action of the rider's seat and legs which should drive the horse towards a more and more restraining but allowing hand. By this intermediate stage the halt should be almost instantaneous, but not abrupt.

## THE REIN BACK
### (PART ONE, CHAPTER 4.8)

**47**   The horse moves backwards, raising and setting down his legs in almost simultaneous diagonal pairs, each foreleg being raised and set down

**28.** *Diagram of figures used during flatwork.*

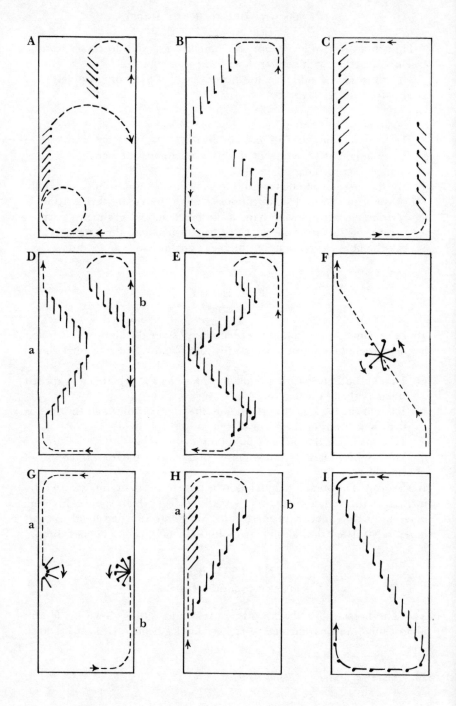

just before the corresponding diagonal hind leg.

THE AIMS:

a   To lift the feet off the ground so the limbs are not dragged;

b   To remain straight;

c   To remain on the bit and ready to move forward;

d   The hind legs should be quite close together and well engaged under the body so that his back does not become hollow.

TO EXECUTE: The rein back should not be asked for before the horse has become reasonably supple, flexible in his joints and off his forehand, otherwise he will find it difficult and will have to be pulled back, which usually leads to a hollowing of the back and further resistances. If the horse does not respond despite being ready to learn to rein back, then the rider instead of pulling back should push onto a stronger contact.

THE STAGES ARE:

a   To practice frequent smooth transitions to the halt, with the horse standing four square and remaining on the bit;

b   After a further good halt, apply the aids to move forward but with the hands restrain the forward movement. As the horse steps back lighten the contact as a reward, but still keep him on the bit.

c   One or two steps are sufficient in the early stages.

d   After stepping back the horse must be rewarded and when asked to walk forward, should do so without hesitation.

e   The rider must control each backward step and vary the number for which he asks.

## THE COUNTER-CANTER
### (PART ONE, CHAPTER 4.18)

**48**   The rider asks the horse to lead with the outside instead of the inside foreleg so that when circling to the left the horse canters with the right lead.

THE AIMS:

a   To maintain the bend to the leading leg so the horse looks to the outside of the circle;

b   To keep the hindquarters from swinging to the outside of the circle;

c   To maintain the rhythm and therefore balance.

TO EXECUTE: The rider should only ask according to the suppleness and collection of his horse and always bear in mind that the conformation of the horse does not allow him to be bent to the line of the circle. The early lessons can consist of loops off a straight line (*see* fig. 28), and then progress as a, b,

**29.** *Diagram of figures incorporating lateral work.*

and c are maintained to circles and serpentines.

BENEFITS:

a   An important suppling and balancing exercise.

b   Encourages the engagement of the hindquarters if done correctly.

c   Can be of use when teaching the flying changes.

# THE SIMPLE CHANGE OF LEG
## (PART ONE, CHAPTER 4.19)

**49** The leading leg at the canter is changed by making a downward transition to walk and after two or three walk steps, the canter re-established with the other leg leading.

THE AIMS:

a   To execute the movement smoothly.

b   To remain on the bit.

c   To maintain impulsion.

d   To keep the hindquarters engaged.

# THE FLYING CHANGE OF LEG
## (PART ONE, CHAPTER 4.19)

**50** This takes place during a period of suspension in the canter when both fore and hind legs should change together, the leading hind leg initiating the change.

THE AIMS:

a   To remain light, calm and straight.

b   To maintain impulsion.

c   To maintain the same rhythm and balance.

d   To achieve a noticeable and clean jump from one leading leg to the other (i.e. the change has expression).

The flying change should not be attempted before:

a   The horse's hindquarters are strong.

b   The horse has the ability to collect at the canter and maintain impulsion.

c   The horse is balanced and straight.

d   The horse remains 'on the bit' during his work.

PREPARATION: He should be made to do simple changes at short intervals on alternate legs. When these are well performed with a degree of collection, the horse remaining straight and 'on the aids', the trainer should ask for alternately true and false canters through the walk.

TO EXECUTE: To make the first flying change as easy as possible for the horse, he is usually cantered across the school on a diagonal in a well balanced, well collected canter and asked to change at the end of the diagonal. If the change has been correctly made the horse should first be settled before being rewarded with a walk on a long rein. If the change was not correct or not made at all, the rider might try once more and, if again it is a failure, he should return to the preparatory exercises before retrying. It is essential that the change should not be late behind, i.e., the change is made first with the forelegs and then a stride or more later with the hind legs. Unless the rider can feel such an error from the saddle, he should have an assistant on the ground to tell him whether the change has been correctly performed.

ALTERNATE SITUATIONS TO ASK FOR A CHANGE: Although most trainers teach their horses flying changes at the end of a diagonal, some horses find the following situations easier positions from which to change. If, therefore, the horse does not change correctly at the end of the diagonal, the positions below can be tried. Also, when continuing the training it is vital that a horse does not anticipate and start to change of his own accord. Therefore, ask for the change from different positions.

THE ALTERNATIVES:

a   From the counter-canter which can be executed down the long side of the school. To prevent anticipation the rider should sometimes continue in the counter-canter beyond the points where he usually asks for a change. It is most important that the horse should remain straight throughout the movement and avoid any sideways drift. It is important too, that the horse changes on the aids and does not anticipate.

b   From the canter half-pass allow one or two straight strides then ask for the change.

c   In a serpentine ask for the change when crossing the centre line.

d   From a 10 or 15 metre (33 or 50 ft) half-circle ask for the change when just about to return to the track.

## LATERAL WORK

**51**   In lateral work the horse moves sideways as well as forwards. This helps to:

a   Increase the obedience of the horse.

b   Supple the horse, increasing the freedom of the shoulders, mobility of the hindquarters and the elasticity of that vital bond connecting the hindquarters, back neck, poll and the mouth.

c   To improve the cadence and balance.

d   To help engage the hindquarters and so increase collection.

THE AIMS:

a   Paces to remain free and regular.

b   To maintain impulsion, rhythm and balance.

c   To achieve a uniform bend from the poll to the tail (except leg yielding when the horse is only bent at the poll). The amount of bend depends on the suppleness and stage of training of the horse. It must never be so excessive (i.e., rider preoccupied with going sideways) that fluency, balance and impulsion are inhibited.

## LEG YIELDING
### (PART ONE, CHAPTER 4.12)

**52**   In the leg yield the horse is straight, except for a slight bend at the poll, allowing the rider to see the eyebrow and nostril on the inside. This bend is in the opposite direction to that which he is moving. The inside legs pass and cross the outside legs.

It is the easiest of the lateral movements requiring no collection and is, therefore, especially valuable in the training of young horses. It is used by many trainers as a means of introducing lateral work but it is a movement which has caused controversy and not all trainers are in agreement with its use. (*See* figs 8 and 29a.)

TO EXECUTE: The first lessons are best given at the walk and only when the horse understands the aids should it be tried at the trot. The usual figures for trying the leg yield are:

a   From a 10 metre (33 ft) circle leg yield out to either the long side of the arena or to start a 20 metre (22 yd) circle.

b   From the short side of the arena turn down the centre line and leg yield to the long side.

c   Along the diagonal when the horse should be as close as possible parallel to the long side but with the forehand just in advance.

d   Along the wall when the horse should not be at a greater angle than 35° to the direction which he is moving.

## SHOULDER-IN
### (PART ONE, CHAPTER 4.14)

**53**   In the shoulder-in the horse moves at an angle of about 30° to the direction of the movement, with the whole horse bent slightly, but uniformly, from the poll to the tail around the rider's inside leg, while looking away from the direction in which he is moving. The horse's inside foreleg passes and crosses in front of the outside leg; the inside hind leg is placed in front of the outside leg. It can be executed on straight lines or circles. (*See* figs 8 and 29a.)

BENEFITS: The shoulder-in is at the very foundation of all lateral work. Because of this, it is perhaps the most valuable of all exercises available to the trainer:

a   It is a suppling and collecting movement as the inside hind leg has to be brought well under the body and placed in front of the outside. To do this the horse must lower his inside hip and flex the joints of the hind leg.

b   It helps the rider to control the shoulder of the horse. By 'thinking shoulder-in' when riding turns and circles, and particularly before striking off to canter, it helps to prevent the shoulder falling out or the quarters coming in.

c   It helps to make the horse straight.

d   It improves the quality of the paces.

e   It can be used to discipline a horse.

AIMS:

a   To maintain impulsion and willingness to go forward.

b   To maintain rhythm.

c   For the bend to be uniform through the whole body and not just the neck, otherwise the collecting value is lost and the shoulders tend to fall out.

d   That the hindquarters do not swing out (that is quarters out instead of shoulder-in).

e   That the movement itself goes 'through' the horse, that is the elastic bond between the hindquarters and mouth is maintained at all times.

TO EXECUTE: Sometimes a first lesson is given at the walk but as soon as the horse understands what is wanted, the movement should be executed at the trot.

The usual way to begin the movement is on completion of a corner before the long side of the school; instead of riding down the long side the rider continues on the curve of the corner bringing the forehand away from the track but keeping the hind legs still on the track where they should remain throughout the movement. The rider when guiding the forehand off the track increases the momentum of his inside leg and the restraining action of the outside rein, while maintaining the bend with the inside rein and controlling the hindquarters with the outside leg.

At first, only a few steps of shoulder-in should be asked for, followed by the horse being ridden forward on a single track in the direction he was facing. The number of steps can be increased as performance and suppleness improve.

## THE TRAVERS AND RENVERS
### (PART ONE, CHAPTER 4.15)

**54**  In the travers (quarters-in) and the renvers (quarters-out) (*see* figs 8 and 29C), the horse is slightly bent around the inside leg of the rider and positioned at an angle of about 30° to the line of the track. They differ from the shoulder-in in that the horse looks in the direction in which he is moving. They can be performed along the wall or centre line.

BENEFITS:

a   To increase obedience;
b   To prepare for the half-pass;
c   To increase the control over the hindquarters;
d   As a collecting exercise in the canter when they can be used in the preparation for the pirouette.

TO EXECUTE: The early lessons are usually given in the walk, but can later be done at trot and canter. To execute travers, at the end of the short side instead of straightening onto the track the bend of the turn is maintained and the aids for travers applied.

The renvers being an inverted travers uses the same muscles, etc., as the travers. It is usual to teach this on the centre line.

## THE HALF-PASS
### (PART ONE, CHAPTER 4.16)

**55**  This is a variation of travers which is executed on the diagonal. (*See* figs 8 and 29d and e.) The horse is slightly and uniformly bent around the inside leg of the rider and should be aligned as nearly as possible parallel to the long side of the school, but with the forehand slightly in advance of the hindquarters. The outside legs cross and pass in front of the inside legs. The horse looks forward and sideways in the direction in which he is moving.

AIMS:

a   To maintain the same balance and rhythm throughout the movement.
b   To maintain a bend but only insofar as impulsion is not lost.
c   To ensure the forehand is light so that there is freedom and mobility in the shoulders and ease and grace to the movement.

TO EXECUTE: Correct execution depends greatly on how the horse goes into the movement and how well the forward element predominates. The trainer might begin the lesson with a half-volte followed by the half-pass. (*See* fig. 29Db.) A useful alternative is shoulder-in along the short side and, as the corner is turned, to go into half-pass across the diagonal, or to leg yield from the centre line to the long side and return to the centre line in half-pass.

## HALF-PIROUETTE AT THE WALK
### (PART ONE, CHAPTER 4.17)

**56** This is a half circle performed on two tracks with a radius equal to the length of the horse. The forehand moves around the haunches. The fore feet and the outside hind foot move around the inside hind foot, which acts as the pivot, returning to the same spot or just in front of it each time it is lifted.

AIMS:
a   Horse should be slightly bent to the direction in which he is moving.
b   To remain on the bit.
c   To maintain the rhythm of the walk.
d   Horse should not move backwards.

TO EXECUTE: The horse can be taught to respond to the aids for the walk pirouette by at first asking him for renvers on a small circle. As he manages to retain the impulsion and sequence of the walk footfalls as the size of the circle can be reduced until it becomes a walk pirouette. (*See* fig. 29Gb.)

## INTRODUCTION OF THE DOUBLE BRIDLE

**57** The double bridle puts finishing touches, or the final polish, on movements which have already been taught and well executed when ridden in a snaffle. It can be worn after the horse has been introduced to lateral work and is accepting the bit in all work. Its first introduction should be with some simple work on a single track. Variations of pace within a gait will help to establish good impulsion and encourage the trainer to ride the horse onto the bit.

The frequency of the use of the double bridle depends upon the rider and the horse.

## SUMMARY

**58** When the horse is able to perform well all the school movements of the Intermediate stage the horse should be a very good ride. It is a level of training which would benefit show jumpers; advanced event horses have to be able to do the work (except flying changes) in order to perform the FEI Three-Day-Event Test. More advanced training on the flat is not important for show jumpers or eventers, so the next chapter is usually treated as the sphere of the specialist dressage horse.

# CHAPTER FIVE

# Advanced Training on the Flat

## INTRODUCTION

1   At this stage the rider/horse partnership begins to specialise. If dressage has been chosen, ultimately 'The dressage rider is an artist and the horse is his medium; together they produce a work of art' (Hans Handler). Only the great riders and horses can achieve this, but it should still be the aim of everybody embarking on this advanced training.

2   **The more particular aims** at this stage should be to train the horse to be:
a   Responsive to delicate aids.
b   Exceptionally supple in all paces and movements.
c   Able to generate great impulsion and collection.

3   **To achieve these the rider must become**:
a   An analyst who pays great attention to detail and is quick to recognise faults and problems.
b   Open minded – ready to admit an error, eager to learn and, if necessary, willing to adjust his means of achieving the ends.
c   Dedicated and able to work with enthusiasm day after day.
d   Aware that no horse can perfect his movements unless he is skilfully ridden. The rider's balance, posture and correct application of aids become critical and can only be developed and maintained through great determination and discipline.

## FACILITIES

4   At this stage regular work is vital. This should be on good going, as hard, rough ground jars the horse and stiffens his back. It is also important that there is enough space to develop the extensions. Therefore, either a large indoor school or outdoor arena (if possible, 20 metres (22 yds) × 60 metres (66 yds) becomes a practical necessity.

## ASSISTANCE

**5** Help from a knowledgeable person on the ground is vital, not necessarily every day, but regularly, to check the rider's position and the horse's paces and movements.

## HORSEMANSHIP

**6** Attention to detail includes the care of the horse, who needs:
a To be well fed as he must be very fit to do advanced work.
b Consistent grooming to keep him clean and to tone up his muscles.
c Constant attention to his physical well-being as strains, sores, etc., if not put right, will affect his work.

## OBJECTIVES OF TRAINING

**7** The objectives remain the same as in the previous chapter, paragraphs 6 to 25, although some should be closer to achievement than others. Thus, the horse by this stage, should be submissive, straight, accepting the bit and able to establish a rhythm, and the major areas for improvement here will be:
a Suppleness (Chapter 4.12),
b Impulsion (Chapter 4.7),
c Collection (Chapter 4.4f and Chapter 1.19).

## GENERAL SCHOOL WORK

**8** With the exception of the turn on the forehand and leg yielding, all the exercises of the Intermediate stage should be included in this basic school work.

**9** **The Paces**: More time can be spent on the walk to develop the variations within this basic pace. The collected and extended walk must be developed, but with great care. An assistant on the ground should check that the sequence of footfalls remains true, for the rhythm is all too easily lost with so little impulsion being produced at the walk.

Greater variations within the trot and canter should be asked for, but taking care to develop enough impulsion to make this possible without hurrying in the extensions, or slowing down in the collections.

**10  The circles**: Ridden at the collected trot and canter can be gradually reduced in size from 10 metres (33 ft) diameter to 6 metres (20 ft) diameter (a volte).

THE AIMS:
a   The hindquarters should not swing inwards or outwards.
b   To avoid excessive bend in the neck.
c   Horse and rider should not lean in (or out).
d   Rhythm is maintained during and when entering and leaving the circles.
e   To perform circles equally well on both reins.

**11  Serpentines**: Should by now be relatively easy suppling exercises at the collected or working trot, and useful variations can be used at the canter. Loops can be performed at the counter-canter as well as true canter, and the width of the loops can be reduced as the horse becomes more collected, so that the exercise becomes progressively more difficult; i.e., use a four loop serpentine in a 20 metre (22 yd) × 60 metre (66 yd) arena at first and then progress to six loops. Flying changes can be executed on the centre line of the serpentine; however, it is also a most useful suppling exercise to do simple changes.

THE AIMS:
a   The loops to be of a similar size and shape.
b   Simple or flying changes to be executed fluently.
c   Rhythm to be maintained.
d   Correct bend to be maintained.

**12  Transitions**: The following direct transitions can be practised:
UPWARD TRANSITIONS:
a   Halt to collected trot.
b   Rein back to collected trot or canter.
c   Collected walk to collected canter.
d   Halt to collected canter.
and later
e   Piaffe to collected trot.
f   Piaffe to passage.
DOWNWARD TRANSITIONS:
a   Extension to collection at all three gaits.
b   Collected walk, collected canter, and medium trot to halt.
and later
c   Passage or piaffe to halt.
THE AIMS:
As in Chapter 4.33.

## LATERAL WORK

**13**  The half-pass, travers and renvers should be executed with a greater degree of sideways movement, but only insofar as the essential forward flow is maintained.

**14  The counter change of hand** (zig zag) is a series of half-passes either side of the centre line. (*See* fig. 29e.)

TO EXECUTE AT THE TROT: From a half-pass to the right the rider's outside leg (left) is used to direct the hindquarters slightly further over to the right and at the same time the horse's bend is changed so that the forehand can take the lead. The aids are then applied for a half-pass to the left.

TO EXECUTE AT THE CANTER: From a half-pass to the right the rider stops driving the horse laterally and rides him straight forward for two or three strides, during which time he asks for the change and the new bend to the left before applying the aids for the half-pass left. When the horse can perform the change fluently and equally well from right to left half-pass or vice versa, then the number of straight strides can be reduced to ultimately one, when the new bend is asked for during the change.

THE AIMS:

a   The forehand must always lead in the half-pass.

b   The horse must take strides of equal length in both directions of the half-pass.

c   Impulsion, rhythm and balance must be maintained throughout the movement.

## FLYING CHANGES IN SERIES
### (PART ONE, CHAPTER 4.19)

**15**  When the horse can execute single flying changes 'on the aids' and in balance he should be ready to start a series of changes when flying changes are executed regularly after a given number of strides. The number of strides between changes can be reduced as he masters the easier series from, say, five to two (two-time changes) and finally to changes every stride (one-time changes).

TO EXECUTE: In these series the degree of collection should be slightly less than in the collected canter to ensure a good forward bound at each change.

One particular series should not be practised for too long, as the horse then tends to anticipate and will not change on the aids. The series and the number of changes asked in any series should be varied.

If teaching a more difficult series, end the lesson on one that is easy for him, that is, four times after doing some two or one times.

THE AIMS:

a   To keep the horse straight. Any tendency to drift or swing should be corrected by:

    ı   Guiding the forehand, thinking shoulder-in, as each change is asked for.

    ıı   Increasing the impulsion, riding forward into the changes at closer to medium canter, and using the inside leg to achieve this.

b   For the change to be executed with the forelegs and hind legs changing simultaneously. If the change is late behind this is usually due to the horse being on his forehand, more impulsion and collection needs to be generated.

c   Rhythm and impulsion must be maintained. If the horse gets slower and slower through the series he should be ridden forward and asked to change at a medium canter. If he gets faster and faster, half-halts should be applied during the strides when he is not changing.

## PIROUETTE AT THE CANTER
### (PART ONE, CHAPTER 4.17)

**16**   The pirouette (half-pirouette) is a circle (half circle) performed on two tracks with a radius equal to the length of the horse. The forehand moves around the hindquarters, the forefeet and the outside hind foot moving around the inside hind foot which is lifted and put down again on the same spot, or slightly in front of it.

THE AIMS:

a   The horse to remain 'on the bit' with a light contact and a slight bend to the direction in which he is turning.

b   To maintain balance, rhythm and impulsion.

c   To maintain the regularity of the canter hoof beats. The inside hindleg is lifted and returned to the ground in the same rhythm as the outside hind foot and should not remain on the ground.

d   The strides should be accentuated, cadenced and for a full pirouette should be six to eight in number and for a half-pirouette three to four.

TO EXECUTE: The pirouette at the canter is one of the most difficult of all the advanced movements to execute correctly, as it calls for a high degree of collection and great impulsion. Horses should only be taught pirouettes after they have developed a good collected canter full of impulsion, responded correctly to the half-halt and are able to shorten the canter so much that for a few strides they almost remain on the spot (still in three-time) before willingly going forward again.

VARIOUS METHODS:

a   From a large walk pirouette and one in which the hindquarters are very well engaged, strike off into the canter while maintaining the same aids as for the walk pirouette. The horse should do a few steps of canter pirouette before cantering straight forward (if he lacks impulsion) or returning to the walk (if he becomes excitable). The success of this method depends on the strike off being of high quality.

b   From the renvers. At the end of a long side the rider asks for a very small half circle (or passade) to canter in renvers parallel to the long side, and then turns towards the wall to perform a three-quarter pirouette. This method enables better control over the outside hind leg at the moment of starting the pirouette (one of the commonest faults is for the hindquarters to swing outwards). Also, the horse is already in the correct bend. (*See* fig. 30.)

c   From a large circle. This can be more difficult, as it is not so easy to prevent the hindquarters falling out, but is a useful progression after methods a and b towards a pirouette on a single track. Voltes are performed within the large circle, eventually making them so small they become a passade and finally, a half-pirouette. Then proceed in counter-canter before trying on the other rein.

d   From travers on a large circle, or from half-pass.

e   From a straight line, but this should not be tried until the horse performs a satisfactory pirouette in the above methods. The rider should give his horse a slight shoulder-in position when approaching the point to which the pirouette is to be carried out, and the canter super collected so that he is almost cantering on the spot when he is asked to turn into the pirouette. (*See* fig. 29f.)

If during attempts at the pirouette, the horse falls into the walk then it is important to keep asking with the aids for the pirouette, but with more vigour so that he returns to the canter. If he starts to swing around quickly, to swivel on his inside hind leg, then return to work at the travers or renvers so that control over every collected stride can be maintained. Also, he can be brought back to the walk during the pirouette, perform a few steps of the pirouette at walk and then strike off into the canter, still in the pirouette

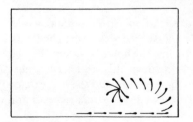

**30.** *Diagram of use of passade and renvers to perform a canter pirouette.*

when more control over each stride should have been established.

It is vital that during the pirouette the rider retains the correct position, that he remains upright with his seat in the saddle and does not tip forward or to the outside with the momentum of the movement.

When working on the pirouettes it is important to remember that they are demanding of the horse and should not be attempted for too long. It is important too that the size of the pirouette is varied from half to three-quarter to whole, so that the horse remains on the aids and ready to come out of it whenever asked.

**17   The Piaffe** (Part One, Chapter 4.20).
This is a highly collected, elevated and cadenced trot on the spot.
THE AIMS:
a   The height of the toe of the raised foreleg should be level with the middle of the cannon bone of the other foreleg. The toe of the raised hindleg should reach just above the fetlock joint of the other hindleg.
b   The neck should be raised and arched, the head perpendicular, the back supple and swinging, and the hindquarters slightly lowered with active hocks well engaged to give great freedom, lightness and mobility to the shoulders and forehand.
c   Each diagonal pair of legs is raised and returned to the ground alternately with an even rhythm and a definite, but short period of suspension.
d   The piaffe is produced as a result of great impulsion so the horse should be ready and willing to move forward at all times.
e   The horse should not move backwards, cross the forelegs, swing the forehand, or hindquarters, or take irregular steps.
f   The horse should remain 'on the bit' with a supple poll and a light but taut rein.
TO EXECUTE: The piaffe can be taught either from the ground or from the saddle. In the former method it is easier for the horse to use his back without the weight of the rider, but some find the latter easier to understand.

**18   Teaching from the ground**: These lessons should take place in a closed arena and the stages are as follows
a   The horse is brought to the middle of the arena, fitted with a snaffle, saddle, cavesson, lunge rein and side reins. The side reins should be adjusted so that they just make contact when the horse is collected and it may be necessary to shorten them to achieve this as he gets more collected. The lunge rein is attached to the cavesson and the horse taken to the track on the left rein as this is the easiest for most horses and convenient for the trainer.

b   The trainer positions himself near the shoulder of the horse; taking up a fairly short rein in his left hand and holding the whip in his right hand he walks the horse slowly once or twice around the arena. As soon as the horse is walking in a calm and relaxed manner, he can be asked to trot. The hind legs should initiate this transition and the steps should be short. If the horse tries to go forward too much the trainer should apply restraining aids with the hand. If the horse is reluctant to go forward, touch him with the whip just above the hind fetlocks. The voice should be used to supplement these driving and restraining aids. When the horse can work calmly and with rhythm in this exercise, the teaching of piaffe can begin.

c   With the horse standing correctly at halt on a long side of the arena, the trainer should position himself, as before, alongside the shoulder of his horse with his whip in his right hand. He will now take up a very short rein, holding his left hand closely behind the head of his horse. (*See* fig. 31.) From the halt the horse should be asked to move forward with a few steps of very collected trot and then brought again to the halt; this time the trainer should move to stand directly in front of his horse. The pupil will soon come to understand that trainer at his side means activity, and trainer in front means immobility.

**31.** *Teaching a horse piaffe from the ground.*

Eventually the aim must be for the horse to work on both reins, but for the first day the trainer may be satisfied with a few good steps on one rein. Over a series of lessons the trainer should progressively ask the horse to shorten the trot strides and increase the collection. The hind-legs must come further under the body and to encourage them to do so and spring elastically off the ground the trainer can use the whip to touch the hind legs just above the fetlocks. Only a few strides a time should be asked for in this manner.

d   When seven or eight perfectly level steps can be executed without moving forward further than one yard, the horse may be ridden, but with the rein still in the hands of the trainer who continues to control the horse from the ground in the same manner as before. Eventually, the trainer can ride the horse to perfect the movement.

THE TRAINER'S MAIN CONSIDERATIONS SHOULD BE:

a   Never to ask too much. The horse has to work hard to produce the necessary impulsion and bouncy spring to his action, so the lessons should not last too long and end if possible, on a good, calm note.

b   The horse must remain straight and if he tries to bring his hindquarters from the wall, the trainer should counter with a slight shoulder-in position.

c   The strides must be level. The trainer should never sacrifice levelness in efforts to produce more elevated steps.

d   The horse should always move forward if only one inch per step, until training has reached its final stage, when 10 to 12 steps on the spot will be the aim.

e   The hind legs should not be brought too far under the body or the hindquarters will be over-burdened; the horse will have difficulty in lifting his hind feet off the ground which tends to make the trot irregular and the forward transitions abrupt.

**19   Teaching from the saddle**: This method, although usually easier for the trainer, since he should have more control, is more difficult for the horse to use his back elastically.

The principle considerations and progressive training methods are similar to those outlined in training from the ground. An assistant trainer walks alongside the horse's hindquarters. The rider applies the aids for piaffe and the assistant, if necessary, taps with the whip to encourage the horse to flex his hind legs and place them further under his body. As soon as the horse steps correctly with diagonal pairs, and the forelegs rise higher than the hind legs, then he can be asked to perform this work more energetically. The collection to achieve this needs to be built up so that just before asking for piaffe-like steps, walk pirouettes and transitions from a shortened trot to halt (and vice versa) can be performed.

If the horse is naturally short of impulsion, the passage might, with advantage, be taught before the piaffe, not only to improve the impulsion but to teach the horse to spring energetically off the ground.

# PASSAGE
## (PART ONE, CHAPTER 4.21)

**20** This is a very collected, very elevated and very cadenced trot. Each diagonal pair of feet is raised higher and with a longer period of suspension than for any other trot.

THE AIMS:

a The toe of the raised foreleg should be level with the middle of the cannon bone of the other foreleg. The toe of the raised hindleg should be slightly above the fetlock joint of the other hindleg, i.e., as in piaffe.

b The neck should be raised and arched with the poll as the highest point and the head close to the perpendicular. The horse should remain on the bit accepting a light contact.

c The hindquarters should be well engaged and the flexion of the knees and hocks should be accentuated, but with graceful elasticity of movement.

d The impulsion should be lively and pronounced and the horse should be able to go smoothly from the passage to the piaffe and vice versa, without apparent effort and without altering the rhythm.

e The steps should be regular and neither the forehand nor the hindquarters should swing from one side to the other.

TO EXECUTE: The passage is taught usually from the saddle and developed out of the piaffe, the collected trot, or sometimes the walk. It depends on the abilities and temperament of the horse, but it is most usual to teach from the piaffe, as long as the horse has mastered this movement.

The horse is ready to be taught passage when he is capable of great collection, extension and of containing his impulsion.

An assistant on the ground might be useful as he can come close to the hindquarters, with a long whip if necessary, and without upsetting the horse indicate that more impulsion and elevation is required.

The rider applies his legs, the pressures being in the rhythm of the passage and sits deep, using the forward driving influence of his seat (Part One, Chapter 3.9 and 10). The hands restrain saying 'no faster' so that the increased impulsion goes upwards to produce passage – the elevated steps gaining little ground. When passage-like steps are achieved they should be maintained just long enough for the horse to understand that this is what is required (3 to 10) and then given a reward.

The rider can reduce the pressure of his legs when the horse goes into passage and cease the pressure when he wants the horse to return to trot.

MAIN CONSIDERATIONS:

a   As with piaffe, regularity in all its aspects is of prime importance; only when this can be achieved and maintained should the trainer strive for greater elevation.

b   The movement should be smooth and flowing; without jerky prop-like landings of the forelegs, or hollowing of the back.

c   Care must be taken that the long whip, used to stimulate activity by applying it to the hindquarters, is not employed too much or too often, so that its stimulating effect is lost.

VARIATIONS OF PASSAGE: Each horse has his characteristic natural type of trot and this should appear in his piaffe and passage. This is why there is so much variation in the types of passage performed. Ideally, the speed of the rhythm (tempo) remains the same in trot, piaffe and passage, but this is rarely possible. In the passage the steps are more elevated and the periods of suspension longer than in either trot or piaffe, so the tempo is usually slower.

## DRESSAGE COMPETITIONS

**21**   Most serious riders aim to compete in dressage competitions and to do so successfully the following are some of the most important considerations:

a   To have a relaxed horse at the competitions, which usually entails frequent visits to shows, whether competing or not, especially with high-spirited, temperamental or young horses.

b   Careful organisation of the 'riding in' period, taking into account the character and abilities of the horse and the test to be performed. The work to be included (lungeing, walking around, loosening up, etc.) and the time it will take should be planned beforehand.

c   Study of judges' sheets to ascertain the defects which need most attention and then to train accordingly.

d   Development of 'arena craft' which entails careful study of the test to be performed, accurate execution of it, good use of the arena (going well into the corners, etc.) and determination to show off the horse at his best.

CHAPTER SIX

# Training the Horse to Jump

## INTRODUCTION

**1**  Horses are born with varying degrees of ability to jump. The trainer's task is to develop the horse's ability giving him the confidence to jump many different types of obstacles and to do so when carrying a rider.

## TO JUMP

**2**  A horse, jumping correctly from a balanced, calm, yet energetic approach, appears to do so with ease. During the last few strides of the approach to an obstacle he stretches his head and neck forward and downwards, then raises them to spring upwards off his forehand; this takes place a moment before the hind feet meet the ground. The powerful muscles of the hindquarters and thighs, and the leverage of the hips, stifles, hocks and fetlocks, push the horse upwards and forwards over the obstacle.

During take-off and over the obstacle, the horse's back should be rounded, not hollow, with the withers as the highest point and with the head and neck stretched forward to help his balance (known as basculing). (*See* fig. 24.) On descent, the head and neck rise slightly and the forelegs meet the ground one after the other, followed by the hindlegs.

This style is the most efficient method of jumping, demanding least effort from the horse, but takes time to build up the muscles and to develop the suppleness to enable him to jump in this way. Rushed training usually results in incorrect muscle development, less efficient styles (e.g., a hollow back in mid-air) and often eventually, because it takes an effort to jump, a loss of confidence and refusal.

**3**  **The muscles which should be developed** through flat work, riding out, especially up and down hills, gymnastic jumping exercises, are as follows:
a   The upper neck muscles, *not* those on the underside.
b   The shoulder and forearm.
c   Back and loin, which are probably the most important.
d   Second thigh muscles.

## THE TRAINING PROGRAMME

**4**  The work for at least the first year of the horse's ridden life is common to an eventer, jumper and dressage horse. He should be broken in as described in Chapter 3, and trained on in the way described in Chapter 4, the Preparatory Stage.

The flat work is vital in order to develop the correct muscles and the controlled riding necessary to jump in the above style, but in the case of the potential show jumper, greater emphasis can be placed on jumping in conjunction with this flat work. Easy obstacles should be used so that he gradually builds up his ability and confidence.

When he is being broken in, and during the early riding days he can be lunged over trotting poles and very small fences. If the facilities are available he could be loose schooled. After he relaxes when ridden, and is sufficiently obedient and fit, the rider can take him over trotting poles, then progressed gradually to small obstacles, with the size and variety of these jumps slowly being increased.

**5**  **The rate of progress** will depend upon the ability of the horse and rider, but the essential factors are that:
a  The jumping should be fun for the horse so he must not be asked too much for his stage of training, nor should he be asked to jump when tired. Schooling sessions over jumps should be short.
b  Slightly more difficult fences may be progressed to when the horse can jump the easier obstacles in the style described in paragraph 2 above, but if at any time he loses his confidence, return to the easier obstacles. It is important that in each jumping lesson he is loosened up over trotting poles and small fences; gradually progressing to ever larger obstacles.

## LUNGEING OVER SMALL OBSTACLES

**6**  The horse first learns to jump without a rider on his back, on the lunge. Starting by walking over a pole on the ground, progress to trotting and then to a series of poles before asking him to jump solid single obstacles. Remember at all times that it is difficult for the horse to jump off the turn and it takes great skill and experience on the part of the lunger to give him the necessary assistance. Therefore, for most trainers it is advisable to restrict the work on the lunge to trotting poles and single obstacles of not more than about 1 metre (3 ft).

**7**  **Techniques of lungeing over obstacles**: *See* Part II, Chapter 2, 21–23.

## LOOSE SCHOOLING OVER OBSTACLES

**8**   If the horse can be made to jump loose, calmly, rhythmically and with impulsion, then this teaches him to look after himself and develop a good style of jumping. Damage can be done with inadequate facilities, and/or inexperienced trainers, resulting in the horse running out, refusing or starting to rush his fences. Like lungeing, loose schooling is only of value if done well.

**9**   **Requirements**:
a   An indoor school or small enclosure from which it is impossible for the horse to escape, or a jumping lane consisting of a series of small fences.
b   If an indoor school or enclosure is used, the obstacles should have wings to discourage the horse from running out.
c   The horse is obedient to aids of the voice and the lunge whip.

**10**   **Techniques**: The horse, wearing a head collar or cavesson and protective boots, should be led around the school once or twice and then let loose and sent round at the trot, driven on when necessary by his trainer's voice and lunge whip.

An assistant is needed and should be responsible for driving the horse forward in one half of the school. The trainer and assistant should never be in front of the horse, as he moves round the track.

When the horse trots calmly and willingly around the school then an obstacle with wings can be erected. It is advisable to place the poles on the ground and only when the horse trots over them confidently should they be raised.

The best position for the obstacle is usually soon after the corner. Placing poles (*see* paragraph 19 below), of 2.60 to 3 metres (8 to 9½ ft), or 5.50 to 6 metres (17½ to 20 ft) in front of the jumps are advisable to stop the horse rushing, or arriving at an awkward take-off position. Alternatively, a pole can be placed diagonally in the corner and the small obstacle 16 metres (52 ft) away from it.

It is vital that the trainer and the assistant present the horse straight at the fence and that they do not chase him into it. It is important that the horse jumps of his own accord, encouraged by the voice and the presence of the whip.

Obstacles should never be 'trappy', nor too high. At a later stage multiple fences may be used.

The horse should be rewarded frequently during loose schooling sessions; after a few good circuits he should be stopped, patted, and occasionally given titbits.

## JUMPING WITH A RIDER

**11** The horse should be ready to jump with a rider only after he has learnt to jump without a rider, has been backed, is fit and responsive to the aids.

## GENERAL PRINCIPLES

**12**

a   It is advisable to have an assistant present when jumping, to put up obstacles, to ensure that the distances between fences are correct and for reasons of safety.

b   The obstacles should be solid or substantial so that the horse does not become careless through finding it easy to hit fences. At the same time, they should be 'inviting' to encourage him to jump and not run out, and kept small enough to prevent him being over-faced.

c   Distances between obstacles and placing and trotting poles should be 'correct' until an advanced training stage.

d   The young horse should be started over fences with which he is familiar and has jumped successfully on the lunge. When trying a strange obstacle it is advisable to make it small in height, to show it to him first and let him sniff at it, and with nervous horses to follow an experienced horse over the fence. At all costs refusals should be avoided.

e   Jumping places a strain on a young horse's tendons and feet; sprains and lameness can be caused, particularly if the ground is too hard, or too soft, or if the horse is not fit enough for the work demanded. Long jumping sessions should be avoided.

**N.B.** There is no need to jump massive fences at home. The aim of trainer is to familiarise the horse with all types of obstacles and to get him going in a style which will make jumping as easy as possible. This can be achieved over low obstacles and even advanced horses need not practice over more than 1.20 metre (4 ft) obstacles.

## METHOD OF RIDING

**13** The rider must be a competent horseman if he is to do this work without hindering his horse. Although remaining in control he should not try to place the horse (adjusting his stride so that he takes off in a particular position).

After presenting his horse straight at the obstacle his aims should be:

a   To sit as still as possible in the correct position.

b  To retain a light rein contact.

c  Although allowing the horse as far as possible to approach and jump the obstacles in his own way, sufficient impulsion is essential and at times the rider might have to generate this with his legs and, if necessary, his seat and taps with the whip. (*See* Chapter 4.8.)

d  The horse will find it easier to jump in the correct style if he approaches the fence in balance, and therefore with rhythm, so that the rider should help his horse to establish a rhythm and not rush or shorten up into a fence.

In the early stages of jump training, the horse should be fitted with a neck strap or a breast plate, as even the most experienced rider may need to hold it or the mane on occasions if he is to avoid interfering with the horse's mouth.

The correct position for the rider is described in Part One, Chapter 1.7 onwards. It is usual with a young horse to adopt the forward seat, out of the saddle, in order to give the horse's back the freedom to work. The seat aids however, can be used momentarily with a horse which tries to stop, or lacks impulsion. When working over trotting poles it is vital that the horse's back can move freely and is not made rigid or hollow. It is usual therefore, to adopt rising trot, although sitting trot is acceptable for a rider with a good seat and a horse which is strong and supple in his back.

## THE STAGES OF TRAINING

**14  Trotting Poles**: Work over poles on the ground, at first singly and then in series, is an essential part of a young horse's general education. It is a useful gymnastic exercise which teaches him to lower his head and neck, to round his back, to flex his joints and also to co-ordinate the action of his limbs.

**15  Distances between poles**: (*See* fig. 32.) Whether on the ground or raised, these must accommodate the horse's stride exactly. For most horses and ponies, except very small ones, the optimum distances are 1.20 to 1.40 metres (4 to 4½ ft) for walking and trotting. This is based on the trotting stride of the average horse, which is about 1.30 metres (4½ ft). It is vital that correct distances are maintained between obstacles, including poles on the ground; the slight adjustments should be made to suit the strides of different horses and the going (heavy needs shorter distances, firm longer). An assistant on the ground should be ready to reposition displaced obstacles, or to adjust distances when they do not suit the stride of the horse.

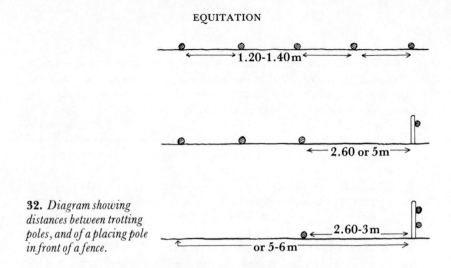

**32.** *Diagram showing distances between trotting poles, and of a placing pole in front of a fence.*

## TO RAISE THE POLES

**16**   These are best put on blocks which have been slightly hollowed out on one side to enable the pole to be fitted and not roll out. Cavalletti can be used as long as the ends are square and heavy. Cavalletti have the advantage of being easy to adjust in height, but those with crossed ends are not advisable as the poles often roll when hit by a horse and can cause accidents. The practice of piling cavalletti on top of each other to form a jump is not recommended for the same reason.

**17**   **Technique**: The horse is firstly walked over a single pole; when he does this calmly, the number can be increased to two, three and then four. With a longer series of poles the horse should tend to trot; if he does not do so then he can be given some encouragement with leg aids.

It is important for the horse to remain calm and maintain a rhythm. If he gets excited then it sometimes helps to remove alternate poles and/or he can be trotted in a circle until he settles, and when he does so the poles can be tried again.

## INTRODUCING OBSTACLES

**18**   When the horse trots over the poles correctly and calmly, a very small obstacle can be erected beyond the last trotting pole. It should look inviting, not exceed 38 cm. (1 ft 3 in.) in height and preferably consist of cross bars which direct the horse towards the centre of the fence. The aim is for the horse to land over the last pole, and to take one stride before taking off for the obstacle. The average horse needs a space of 5 metres (16½ ft) to achieve this. Alternatively, no stride need be taken when the last trotting pole is placed 2.60 metres (8 ft) in front of the fence. These distances should be adjusted for long or short striding horses and ponies.

## PLACING POLES

**19** In order to help the horse arrive at a good position for take-off, especially in the early stages when the rider should not interfere, it is advisable to use either trotting poles as above, or a single placing pole which should be either 2.60 to 3 metres (8 to 10 ft) (no stride), or 5 to 6 metres (16½ to 20 ft) (one stride) in front of the jump.

## TYPES OF OBSTACLES

**20** As soon as the horse can jump a particular fence at the end of a line of trotting poles, or after a placing pole, calmly and in good style then he can be asked to jump a slightly higher, wider, or different type of obstacle in the same manner.

**21** **Single fences**: The horse must gradually be introduced to fences (with groundlines) without trotting poles or a placing pole. The horse should learn to think for himself and adjust his stride, but reversion to use of a placing pole is of value, if a horse starts to rush the fence, for inexperienced riders and for the first few jumps in any lesson.

**22** **Combinations**: The horse must be gradually introduced to series of fences between which he can take one or two strides. These should start very low so that the horse can gain his confidence.

A placing pole is usually advisable in front of a small upright and then a correct distance of 5.60 metres (18 ft) (one stride) or 10 metres (33 ft) (two strides) to a second small upright. As the height of the fences is raised and spreads introduced, these distances should be lengthened to range from 6 to 6.50 metres (20 to 21 ft) (one stride), 10.30 metres (33½ ft) (two strides), for fences not more than .90 metre (3 ft), and up to 8 metres (26 ft) (one stride) and 11 metres (36 ft) (two strides) for the higher fences and when training the horse to take longer strides.

**23** **Grids**: A series of trotting poles and small fences is of use in developing a horse's gymnastic ability. It is advisable to keep the fences under .90 metre (3 ft) and it is vital that the distances are correct. An example would be a series of trotting poles 1.30 metres (4½ ft) apart, the last of which is 2.60 metres (8 ft) from a .60 metre (2 ft) upright which is 3.50 metres (11½ ft) (no stride) from about .90 metre (2 ft 9 ins) upright which is 6.25 metres (20 ft) (one stride) from about .90 metre (2 ft 9 ins) high × about .90 metre (2 ft 9 ins) wide parallel and this is 10.30 metres (33½ ft) (two strides) from about 1 metre (3 ft) high upright.

For the average horse the following distances are correct: (*See* fig. 32.)
a   Trotting poles – 1.30 metres (4½ ft)
b   *No stride* between a trotting pole and a small fence – 2.60 metres (8 ft)
c   *No stride* between two small fences – 3.50 metres (11½ ft)
d   *One stride* between two small fences – 6 to 6.50 metres (20 to 21 ft)
e   *Two strides* between two small fences – 10 to 10.50 metres (33 to 34 ft)


## CANTERING

**24**   The non-jumping strides at the above distances are taken at the canter, but the approach should be at the trot. In the early stages of jump training it is advisable to approach all the fences at the trot as at this pace the horse is usually more balanced and the slower speed encourages him to bascule. Some riders allow their horses to break into the canter just before the obstacle, but it is not advisable to make the entire approach at the canter until the horse's work on the flat at this pace is satisfactory, and the fences are higher than about 1 metre (3 ft 3 ins). At the canter the horse takes in his stride tiny obstacles tending to flatten and failing to develop his bascule.


## CHANGING THE DISTANCES

**25**   When the horse jumps combinations and grids with correct distances, calmly and in a good style, then the distances can be varied, but by inches only at a time, to teach him to jump from both long and short strides. It is best to keep any series of fences either for short strides or for long. Alternating short and long distances is very difficult and inadvisable for all except top horses and riders.


## VARYING THE FENCES

**26**   The horse must be taught to jump all types of fences with confidence.

Consequently, he should be introduced to miniature versions of all the fences found in the show ring – brightly coloured obstacles, walls, triple bars, oxers, planks, brushes, barrels, etc. When riding out every opportunity can be taken to jump the young horse over strange obstacles, such as ditches, banks, hedges, logs, etc., as long as they are low enough not to over-face the pupil.

**27  The water jump** should also come into the training programme. Firstly, he must learn not to fear it, so he can be walked through puddles and made to jump small streams and ditches, preferably following a more experienced horse. The first water jump he is asked to try should not be wide (a maximum of 3 metres [10 ft]). It is also advisable to put a pole of about .90 metre (3 ft) high over the centre of the water as this will encourage him to jump into the air and not just pop over the brush into the water.

The rider should try to get the horse to approach a water with a little more speed than for a normal fence and to ask him to take-off as close as possible to the water.

## COURSES

**28**  A horse which is to compete must learn to jump series of fences other than in straight lines. Therefore, a short course of fences, similar to, but less in number and smaller in height than those in the show ring can be erected. The rider should try to give the horse the best possible approach to the fence so:

a  He must not cut the corners but give the horse as many straight strides before the fence as possible.

b  He must keep the horse balanced and in a rhythm and to do this he will probably need to half-halt and collect his horse immediately he lands over each fence and take great effort to turn each corner correctly.

c  The horse must have enough impulsion (*see* Chapter 4, paragraph 8) to tackle the fences, but impulsion must not be confused with speed – going fast will tend to make the horse flatten over the fences.

## JUMPING AT SPEED

**29**  Most jump offs are against the clock, so any horse and rider having had sufficient training to make winning a possibility must learn how to jump a course in a quick time. Galloping into the fences is rarely advisable with young horses which tend to flatten and become careless. The horse must, therefore, learn to jump fences at angles and to be balanced enough to cut a corner and having taken one or two strides to jump the obstacle.

The rider should aim to maintain impulsion and rhythm when practising these techniques over small obstacles.

## REFUSING

**30** This is a problem which the trainer should try to avoid at all costs. Therefore, never ask a horse to jump a fence higher than he and the rider are capable of. With strange obstacles, give the horse every opportunity to gain his confidence by starting very low, by getting a more experienced horse to jump first, and by making the fence as inviting as possible with a ground line, good width and wings to stop run-outs.

If the horse does refuse, then if it is through lack of confidence or poor riding, lower the fence before trying again. If the horse is doing it out of mischievousness and starting to do it frequently, then he should be reprimanded once, and ridden strongly into the fences.

## RUSHING

**31** (1) **Into the fence**: This makes it difficult for the horse to be balanced and arrive at the correct take-off position. It is often claimed to be due to over eagerness, but on the contrary it is usually due to lack of confidence and the horse trying to get the frightening operation of jumping over as quickly as possible.

TO CORRECT:

a   The rider must give his horse confidence and this is best done by jumping frequently over small single fences, so that it becomes part of the routine rather than a major operation. Consecutive fences should not be attempted. After jumping a fence, settle the horse before attempting another.

b   The rider can circle his horse in front of the fence until he settles into a rhythm, and only then allow him to jump.

c   Trotting poles can be placed in front of the obstacle, and it is usually best to walk into the first pole of the line.

d   Small grids can be used frequently.

e   Jump on a circle with a short approach.

**32** (2) **After the fence**: It is important that the horse is balanced as soon as possible after the fence and does not rush off. If the voice and half-halts (but not pulling on the reins) are not effective then place a pole at either 6.50 metres (21 ft) or 9.50 metres (31 ft) after the fence.

## TAKING OFF TOO CLOSE

**33** Horses which take off too close to the fence lack scope and/or confidence.

TO CORRECT:
a   The horse must be given sufficient impulsion to clear the fence.
b   A take-off rail should be placed about a foot out from the base of each fence.
c   The distances between fences in combinations and grids can be very gradually lengthened so that he learns to extend his stride and to take-off further away.
d   Use of placing poles to get the horse to stand back.

## JUMPING WITH A HOLLOW BACK

**34** Horses tend to jump with a flat or hollow back if they approach the fences too fast and/or take-off far away.

TO CORRECT:
a   Jump fences out of a trot rather than a canter.
b   Use placing poles in front of the fences to encourage him to get underneath the fences. Starting with a distance which is easy for him, gradually shorten it so he has to take-off closer to the fence.
c   Jump plenty of low wide parallels which encourage a horse to bascule and fold the forelegs.
d   Use plenty of grids with relatively short distances between the fences.

## FAMILIARISATION

**35** A horse's first show is usually a nerve-racking experience. It is advisable therefore, to take him to a show before he starts competing and to get him relaxed in this stimulating atmosphere.

# CHAPTER SEVEN

# Cross-Country Training

## INTRODUCTION

**1** To be successful across country the horse must be able to cope with the great range of problems found in today's competitions. Both horse and rider must learn (through careful thorough training and familiarisation) how to approach and jump the variety of fences met in events.

## EARLY TRAINING

**2** **The aims** of early training are to teach the horse:

a  To regulate pace and cope with slopes and all types of going, including entering water.

b  To respect solid fences.

c  To become a safe conveyance across country by being encouraged from the beginning to work things out for himself.

d  To be tough and able to perform in all types of weather – he should not be over 'cosseted'.

**3** **Flat work**: This should continue in the manner described in Chapter 4.

**4** **Jumping exercises**: The horse's athletic ability is built up over a period of months by varying the exercises over trotting poles, grids and small fences, jumped at angles from both trot and canter. At these angled fences the rider must be able to use each hand independently to effectively guide the horse and keep the legs against the horse's sides at all times.

Jumping exercises should be carried out up to two to three times a week in between flat work and hacks.

**5** **Hacking**: Whilst out hacking the horse should learn to cope with all types of going and terrain. He has to be able to balance himself going up and down hills and over rough ground. It is best to use a loose rein as much as possible so that he can think and hold himself without reliance on the rider. Popping over little fences, such as logs and ditches, when out hacking will teach him to be alert and quick thinking. Water should be ridden through and over whenever possible.

It is vital that the horse is never frightened, so:

a   Everything attempted should be within the horse's capabilities for his stage of training.

b   The fence should be safe with good take-offs and landings. A nasty experience in the early stages could undermine a horse's confidence.

**6   Schooling over cross-country fences**: This can start once the horse is confident when jumping fences on flat ground of just over 1 metre (3ft 6 ins), is balanced and controllable enough to jump combinations and is able to lengthen and shorten his stride. Several sessions may be required. The first should be over straightforward fences of different types up to 0.90 metre (3 ft). In the following sessions, start with a few simple obstacles and gradually increase the questions asked by including ditches and rails, steps, banks, bullfinches, rails at varying angles and corners. The horse should be progressively familiarised with the types of fences which are met with on cross-country courses. Always finish on a good note – before the horse gets too tired.

**7   Hunting**: Some horses learn the techniques of cross-country jumping much quicker than others, but all benefit from a season's hunting, teaching both rider and horse to go boldly across country and to think quickly over unfamiliar ground. This is how horses learn to produce a 'fifth leg' and become adept at jumping the unexpected.

**8   Hunter Trials**: Once the horse jumps small cross-country fences confidently, he can be entered in novice hunter trials. Pair classes may benefit the timid horse if a more experienced horse is the pair and leads to give him confidence.

Progression to more advanced competitions depends on how the horse tackles the small ones. As long as he goes well at the lower level, then he can be asked a bit more and the difficulty increased as and when the horse is confident enough to cope. Never ever ask too much at once.

## TYPES OF FENCES

**9**   Cross-country fences can be divided into several categories according to the method of riding needed to negotiate them safely at the faster speed used when cross-country riding.

**10   Respect needed for every fence**: Every type of fence needs treating with respect and all too often it is the 'simple' ones that cause the most trouble. This is usually because more thought goes into approaching and riding the more difficult fences, with the result that they often cause comparatively few problems. The rider must treat each fence as if it is *the* most important one, so that the horse is given the maximum help throughout. Ridden in this way horses build up confidence in their rider and vice versa, and the combination then becomes a partnership, each confident in their ability to jump any course attempted. Confidence is one of the most important aspects of cross-country riding.

**11  Upright**: Uprights should present few problems, although this does depend on how and where they are built. The rider must examine:

a  To see if there is a false ground line (the pole on or nearest to the ground is behind the higher poles). Horse and rider usually judge the take off point by looking at this lowest pole and if they do so when it is a false groundline will get too close to the fence.

b  If the ground is uneven.

c  Whether the fence can be easily seen from the line of approach.

d  The height of the fence.

THE AIM SHOULD BE:

a  To ride straight at the fence in almost all cases.

b  To be accurate, never asking for too much of a stand-off, nor getting too close.

c  To build up plenty of impulsion if the upright is sited on the top of a hill to ensure that the horse's hocks are underneath him before he takes off.

d  If at the bottom of a hill uprights need approaching steadily, making sure the horse is not on its forehand but well between the hand and leg. Then he can take off easily, yet remain balanced on landing.

**12  Spreads**: The aims should be to ride at spread fences

a  With plenty of impulsion. Approaching too slowly will necessitate last minute effort and this could easily frighten a young horse.

b  With care not to let the horse stand off too far and so make the fence unnecessarily wide.

c  If they are sloped spreads they are rarely a problem, so long as the rider does not ask for too big a stand-off and allows the horse as much rein as he needs.

d  If they are parallels they should be ridden at straight and accurately and keeping the horse well between hand and leg, and not on the forehand, as he must get off the ground in time to clear the front rail if he is to avoid disastrous results!

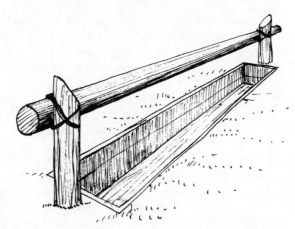

**33.** *A trakehner.*

**13   Ditches and Open Water**: Aims when riding

a   Ditches need riding at strongly, particularly on the 'spooky' type of horse who may tend to have a last minute look.

b   Open water is ridden at strongly, but accurately, encouraging the horse to spring up into the air. Strong legs are applied and a good contact on the reins maintained to keep him up so that he jumps the obstacle clearly. Often the edges to water are a bit soft.

c   Large, wide ditches or 'graves' need very strong riding with legs and sometimes the seat and a good firm contact on the reins, to encourage the horse to go upwards and forwards. They rarely cause trouble when ridden in this way, despite their horrific appearance.

d   Open ditches with brush and with rails always need bold riding.

e   Rails over ditches, trakehners and tiger traps (*see* figs 33 and 34) often

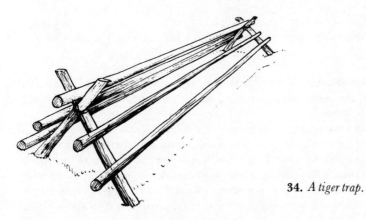

**34.** *A tiger trap.*

cause trouble because the horse (and rider) tend to look down into them and then lose the impulsion to clear the fence. Firm riding with plenty of leg encouraging the horse forward and up in the air is needed, as this fence which although very simple, often causes problems on novice courses.

f   Angled rails over a ditch are generally best approached straight and in the middle, or slightly to the side, where the rail is farthest away, as the ditch acts as a nice ground-line.

**14   Water**: Water needs riding into with a great deal of thought and care.
ASSESSING THE WATERS: It is difficult to judge the pace at which any fence into water is best jumped unless the depth and landing are known. Therefore, before attempting it on horseback try and walk through the water to ensure the base is even, does not have any holes or soft patches, to determine the depth and whether the water is fast flowing or still.
AIMS WHEN RIDING:

a   The approach should not be too fast, as the drag of the water on landing tends to tip the horse onto his forehand. Coming in too slowly however, can cause an unnecessary stop. A good strong trot or 'bouncy canter' is usually the best pace.

b   The horse should be encouraged to jump out as far as possible so that it does not land too steeply.

c   As most water jumps involve some degree of drop the rider adjusts his position to prevent being thrown forward on landing. This helps the horse keep his balance, and enables him to be ridden forward immediately.

d   Fences in water or involving going through water on the approach, are best approached at a trot to avoid too much spray, which can unsight the horse.

Many falls would be avoided if water was ridden at a sensible pace. A definite controlled approach and control on landing are the two vital factors.

**15   Combinations**: All combinations require accurate and controlled riding and the more difficult really test the athletic ability of the horse.
AIMS WHEN RIDING:

a   Rails at varying angles to each other. These need practice at home so that the horse is familiar with all the differing forms of one and two stride distances. (*See* Chapter 6.22.) The line of the approach is of the utmost importance. Once the best line has been determined a straight route through the obstacle is the secret of success. Having decided on the route which will give your horse the best distances, it is vital to arrive at the exact spot for take off. Therefore, a line through the obstacle is determined by going from a certain landmark straight towards another, i.e., from a conveniently situated tree to a certain telegraph pole.

b   Bounces which demand great agility are very difficult for stiff horses. They must be approached steadily, but with plenty of impulsion so that the horse resembles a tightly coiled spring being released over each jump. Approaching this type of obstacle too fast with the horse on the forehand is inviting disaster; controlled forward impulsion should be aimed at. Grid work is the start towards this, but practice over higher fences with wider distances is necessary to teach the horse to use himself properly. Start with fences at approximately 0.80 metre (2 ft 6 in. to 3 ft) at about 3.1 metres (9 ft to 10 ft) distance of 3 to 4.2 metres (10 ft to 14 ft) in between. Practising at home it is best to gradually build up the height and lengthen the distance to suit the striding of each particular horse.

Bounces demand great effort from the horse and should not be over-done. Two or three successful attempts are sufficient and the horse should always be loosened up well before practising this type of exercise.

**16   Coffins**: (*See* fig. 35.) These are fences which catch out the unwary and should be mastered before tackling them in competition.

TO PRACTICE: Once the horse is confident jumping all types of ditches he can be introduced to rails one or two strides immediately after the ditch and then progress to jumping rails in front of the ditch. As soon as he is confident he can be asked to jump rails, ditch, rails, varying the distances of the rails either side of the ditch.

AIMS WHEN RIDING:

a   The approach is all important, but the technique depends on the siting of the fence. The usual siting is downhill to the first section with an uphill last element. Generally, coffins require steady but determined riding as the horse may not see the ditch until the last moment.

b   As the 'out' of the coffin is often uphill and can be rather close to the ditch, the horse must be kept in balance and not allowed to 'launch off' from the bottom and then fail to clear the final element.

c   The position of the rider throughout at such fences is important as if he

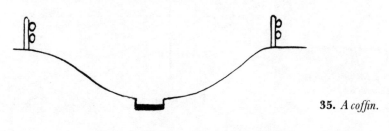

**35.** *A coffin.*

gets too far in front or behind the movement of the horse at the crucial moment he may hinder the horse and prevent him from completing the fence.

## 17 Banks:

AIMS WHEN RIDING:

a   Banks need to be ridden at with great impulsion.

b   They should be approached straight.

c   Once on top of a bank the rider must maintain forward impulsion.

d   On landing, balance the horse by maintaining an upright position and not allowing the legs to move backwards.

e   If a Normandy bank – a bank with rails off – maintain plenty of forward impulsion, especially at those fences designed for an on-off jump. The horse should be allowed to jump out well to avoid a 'peck' landing which may follow if this type of jump is ridden at too slowly.

## 18 Steps and Drops:

AIMS WHEN RIDING:

a   Steps up require enough momentum to overcome the shortening effect of jumping uphill, and the 'push' must be maintained to the top if there are several.

b   Drop fences or steps down, the horse should be steadied so that he does not land with too much impetus which he is then unable to control. The rider should keep the weight upright and off the forehand. Steps down are best approached from trot.

## 19 Corners:

Corners require an accurate, calculated approach and an ability to ride straight. It is safest to choose the line as shown in fig. 36.

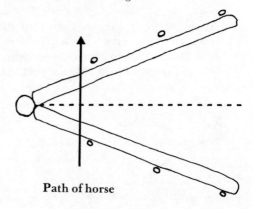

*36. A corner fence showing the safest path for the horse, i.e., at right angles to a line which bisects the corner.*

**Path of horse**

ASSESSING CORNERS: The line of approach must be determined allowing enough room to jump, not too close to the apex and the flag that there is danger of running out, yet not too far in where the fence becomes too wide to jump safely. Study the fence carefully on foot so that the spot to be jumped is clear and then move back from the fence to see the line you wish to approach. Choose a suitable landmark which will not be obscured when riding, that is on the far side and aim to ride at it to ensure the fence is met absolutely right.

AIMS WHEN RIDING: Ride to the landmarks. Take the fence with precision and this will ensure a good ride over a corner fence.

## JUMPING AT SPEED

**20** Cross-country jumping requires a faster speed than for show jumping. The rider should help the horse to negotiate the solid, fixed obstacles by riding sensibly and keeping the horse under control at all times. As the horse gains experience the speed can be increased, but the horse must always be listening and obedient so that he can be balanced for the turns and fences. A good steady rhythm, avoiding unnecessary pulling, and aiming always for the most direct route from one fence to another, is more important than speed and will take less out of the horse.

## THE RIDER'S POSITION

**21** He should be in the galloping position with shortened leathers, the seat out of the saddle and a good contact on the reins. On approaching a fence the horse should be steadied and balanced with the legs. The rider lowers his seat to the degree necessary to maintain the impulsion needed by a particular fence, e.g., steadier at uprights than those with a good ground line. Upon landing, the galloping position should then be resumed.

## GALLOPING

**22** The gallop must be perfected before entering more advanced events. This will also help clear his wind and make him fit. When out hacking, the horse should learn to canter on strongly remaining obedient and calm. It should be remembered that flat out galloping is not required on cross-country courses and it is more important to practise cantering at a strong pace up and down hills and over fences, in the preparation for one-day events. For two- and three-day events the horse should learn to gallop, but it is a mistake to over-gallop a horse as this will wear him out or lame him before getting to the competition!

Galloping should always be done on the best possible ground and, if possible, slightly uphill as this puts far less strain on the horse's legs, while still helping to clear his wind.

Galloping should not be attempted until the horse is fit and has been in serious work at least six to eight weeks. Start with five to six furlong gallop, being careful to keep the horse balanced and well between hand and leg. Begin fairly slowly and then push the horse on for the last quarter mile to make him blow. Bring him back to a walk steadily. Never allow him to flounder along. Loosen the girths and walk until he has cooled off and stopped blowing.

The amount of galloping and distance will depend on each horse, and on the terrains as galloping uphill makes the horse work harder than on the flat.

## INTERVAL TRAINING

**23**  This is becoming a popular alternative to galloping as a means of getting a mature eventer fit. Several short periods of work are alternated with brief recovery periods (the intervals). It is based on methods devised by Jack le Goff and adapted from interval training methods used by athletes.

**24  Principles**:
1  The body will adapt itself to the stress of demands made upon it, provided it is given time. Therefore repeatedly small but increased demands are made upon it.
2  The intervals are timed so that the recovery is not quite achieved before the next period of work.
3  The work periods are designed to avoid maximum stress, so that the respiratory, cardio-vascular and muscular systems are all gradually developed.
4  It is used not more than once every three or four days as it takes this long for the metabolism to return to normal.

**25  Use**: Interval training is only suitable for
a  A mature horse.
b  A sound horse.
c  A horse which has completed 4 to 8 weeks of basic fittening and conditioning work (i.e., capable of hacking for two hours).

**26  Timing**: 6 to 12 weeks of interval training are needed before a three-day event.

**27  The Programme**: A programme is devised so that the distance and speeds are gradually increased and includes approximately two competitions.

Before cantering the horse should be warmed-up by 30 minutes of walking and trotting.

After cantering he should be cooled down by gentle work for up to an hour. This is essential to help the vascular system remove waste products accumulated during exercise.

All work must be done with the horse going into the bridle and on the aids.

**28  An Individual Programme**: It is vital that the programme is adjusted to suit the needs of the individual horse. The aspects which can be varied are

a  *The intervals:* Range of one to four minutes. Four minutes may be needed for the horse to 'almost' recover at the beginning of training but only one minute for a very fit horse.

b  *Work Periods:*

    i  *Duration* Range 3 to 12 minutes, but in total a training session should not be more than 35 minutes. The aim is to work up to cantering at least the distance of the steeplechase and cross country combined. **N.B.** Excitable horses can be cantered for longer distances more slowly.

    ii  *Number:* A maximum of three.

    iii  *Frequency:* Interval training may be used once to twice a week. With a young horse once a week might be sufficient, but it is usual to progress to twice a week.

    iv  *Speeds:* These range from trot to a canter at about 600 metres/minute. Young horses might begin their interval training with trot periods but the majority of work is done at 'half speed' – a canter of approximately 400 m./min. As the horse becomes fitter it can be increased to 500 m./min. and eventually for $\frac{1}{2}$ mile or 1 mile periods at 600 m./min. **N.B.** Horses competing in one- or two-day events before the Three-Day Event need not do faster work until the last two to three weeks. Horses with bad legs should work up hills instead of the faster work, and depending on their 'wind' may need one or two pipe openers going at close to maximum speed for 500 m. uphill 10 days before the event.

    v  *Terrain:* If hilly, distances can be reduced by up to 25 per cent. **N.B.** Varied terrain helps to keep the horse fresh.

c *Work on non-cantering days:* If the horse works strongly for 1½ hours on these days, then less cantering may be needed; if he does not do much, then more may be needed. The work done on these days varies enormously between trainers and is a major cause of differences in cantering programmes.

N.B. After a competition a horse will need usually a minimum of seven days before cantering again.

d *The Horse:* The type of horse and how recently he has been fit affects the programme. A small thoroughbred which has been very fit in the near past needs less work than a cold-blooded horse which has never been really fit.

**29  Evaluating Fitness:**

a *Heart and Respiration Rates:* Heart rates can vary, but once a norm has been established a record of the levels and recovery rates of the heart and respiration help in the evaluation of fitness. For a meaningful comparison the same amount of exercise and the same intervals after work must be taken. One method is to compare rates every 10 days by cantering up the same hill, stopping and taking the rates after one, five and ten minutes. As training progresses the rates should drop.

The pulse at rest is normally between 36 to 44 beats/minute and at maximum is over 200. For maximum training effect the pulse rate should stay between 80 and 150 while the horse is working.

Respiration at rest is normally 10 to 16 and it should not go above 100 during work.

'False' readings can occur as an excited horse has a high pulse and a hot horse can respire very quickly.

Establish a normal pattern for each individual horse in a given situation.

b *Feel:* It is the experienced eye of the trainer and the feel of the rider which judge the fitness of the horse and his best programme of work. There is no substitute for knowing one's horse for he is a unique living animal with his own capabilities, limitations and requirements.

## THE START AND FINISH

**30  Starting** is important as a quick getaway at the start can save valuable seconds. Practise walking into a start box or similar area. Keeping quite calm, walk in a small circle until the starter begins the count-down at five seconds. Quietly face the horse towards the entrance and on the 'go' remember to give with the hands as the horse is urged forwards. The rider should not fight the exuberant horse. He will settle far quicker if the rider sits quite still and keeps a firm contact on the reins.

**31   When finishing** a course, keep hold of the horse's head and bring him gradually back to a walk. Flopping in on a loose rein at speed is foolish as tired horses easily break down if they stumble.

## CARRYING WEIGHTS

**32**   This rarely causes trouble so long as the weight is evenly spread on either side in a weight cloth. The further forward the weight the better, but if carrying a large amount do not put it all on the front. Always remember to pull the weight cloth up under the front of the saddle before tightening the girths, otherwise it can be uncomfortable if allowed to press down on the withers. It is a good idea to practise riding with weights if the horse has not had them before and a few sessions jumping will accustom the horse to the difference if a large amount has to be carried.

## SAFETY EQUIPMENT

**33**   Safety when jumping cross-country cannot be too strongly stressed. Over-reach boots, brushing boots, surcingle and a breast plate are strongly advised with studs being used behind, and in front if the going is slippery. Crash hats are compulsory in Horse Trials and cross-country events.

## SUMMARY

**34**   The need for patience and thoughtful training cannot be stressed too strongly; these are vital in the education of the young horse. If time is spent in the beginning gradually increasing the ability and confidence of the horse, then the outcome should be rewarded by many happy hours riding across country in what is a thrilling and most exciting aspect of equestrian sport.

| Conversion Table for the Typical Event Horse: | |
|---|---|
| 1600 m = 1 mile approx. | ½ speed = 400 m/m approx. |
| 2400 m = 1½ miles approx. | ¾ speed = 600 m/m approx. |
| 3200 m = 2 miles approx. | max speed = 800 m/m approx. |

# A Possible Programme to get a Horse Ready for a Three-Day Event

## THE BASIC CONDITIONING WORK HAVING BEEN COMPLETED.

N.B. *Where speeds not stated simply divide distance by number of minutes; i.e., Week 1 4/1600 m is 400 m/m.*

| Week | Session | Minutes/distance of 1st work period | Minutes of rest | Minutes/distance of 2nd work period | Minutes of rest | Minutes/distance of 3rd work period |
|---|---|---|---|---|---|---|
| 1 | a | 4/1600 m | | | | |
|   | b | 6/2400 m | | | | |
| 2 |   | 4/1600 m | 3 | 4/1600 m | | |
| 3 | a | 4/1600 m | 3 | 6/2400 m | | |
|   | b | 4/1600 m | 3 | 6/2400 m | | |
|   | c | 6/2400 m | 3 | 6/2400 m | | |
| 4 | a | 6/2400 m | 3 | 6/2400 m | 3 | 6/2400 m |
|   | b | 4/1600 m | 3 | 6/2400 m | | |
| 5 | a | 6/2400 m | 3 | 8/3200 m build up to 520 m/m for last 500 m. | | |
|   | b | 6/2400 m | 3 | 8/3200 m 520 m/m for 500 m plus 600 m/m for last 500 m. | | |
| 6 | | One-day Event 3800 m at 520 m/m Cross-country. Rest.* | | | | |

| Day | | Session 1 | No. | Session 2 | No. | Session 3 |
|---|---|---|---|---|---|---|
| 7 | a | 5/2000 m | 3 | 7/2800 m 500 m/m for last 800 m. | | |
| | b | 6/2400 m | 2 | 9/3600 m 600 m/m. | | |
| 8 | a | 6/2400 m | 3 | 6/2400 m 520 m/m. | 2 | 8/3200 m starting at 500 m/m build-up to 650 m/m for last 1600 m. |
| | b | 9/3600 m 570 m/m for 500 m | 2 | 8/3200 m starting 550 m/m 700 m/m. | | |
| 9 | | Two-day Event Steeplechase 3000 m at 690 m/m – Cross-country 5500 m at 570 m/m.* Rest.* | | | | |
| 10 | a | 6/2400 m | 3 | 8/3200 m 550 m/m for last 500 m. | | |
| | b | 7/2800 m | 2 | 9/3600 m 650 m/m. | | |
| 11 | a | 9/3600 m 550 m/m for 800 m. | 2 | 8/3200 m starting 550 m/m building up to 700 m/m for last 1600 m. | 1 | 4/1600 m at 700 m/m. |
| | b | 6/2400 m | 2 | 6/2400 m starting 500 m/m building up to 600 m/m | | |
| 12 | | Pipe-opener day before Endurance Test 500 m uphill at 750 m/m. | | | | |

* More rest days may be necessary according to individual horse.

# Index